SCIENCE

FOUNDATIONS

Gravity

SCIENCE FOUNDATIONS

SCIENCE
FOUNDATIONS

Gravity

PHILLIP MANNING

CHELSEA HOUSE
PUBLISHERS
An imprint of Infobase Publishing

Science Foundations: Gravity

Copyright © 2011 by Infobase Publishing

Chelsea House
An imprint of Infobase Publishing
132 West 31st Street
New York, NY 10001

Library of Congress Cataloging-in-Publication Data
Manning, Phillip, 1936–
  Gravity / Phillip Manning.
      p. cm. — (Science foundations)
  Includes bibliographical references and index.
  ISBN 978-1-60413-296-0 (hardcover)
  1. Gravitation—Popular works. 2. Gravity—Popular works. I. Title.
II. Series.
  QC178.M365 2010
  531'.14—dc22   2010015793

Chelsea House books are available at special discounts when purchased in bulk quantities for businesses, associations, institutions, or sales promotions. Please call our Special Sales Department in New York at (212) 967-8800 or (800) 322-8755.

You can find Chelsea House on the World Wide Web at
http://www.chelseahouse.com

Text design by Kerry Casey
Cover design by Ben Peterson / Takeshi Takahashi
Composition by EJB Publishing Services
Cover printed by Bang Printing, Brainerd, MN
Book printed and bound by Bang Printing, Brainerd, MN
Date printed: December 2010
Printed in the United States of America

10 9 8 7 6 5 4 3 2 1

This book is printed on acid-free paper.

All links and Web addresses were checked and verified to be correct at the time of publication. Because of the dynamic nature of the Web, some addresses and links may have changed since publication and may no longer be valid.

Contents

A Not-So-Simple Concept

G ravity causes objects with **mass** to attract one another. Gravity is what makes rocks fall to the ground; it keeps the Moon and Earth in their orbits; and it is, maybe most incredibly, what makes **black holes** black. However, this seemingly simple concept is not as straightforward as it appears.

Consider, for example, the videos shown on television of astronauts floating around in space outside the International Space Station as it orbits Earth. They float, the television announcer tells viewers, because the space travelers are working in a zero-gravity environment. Yet the gravitational attraction between two bodies is never zero, although the **force** between them decreases as the distance increases. Furthermore, Earth's gravity is strong enough to hold the Moon, which is about 239,000 miles (384,000 kilometers) away, in orbit. So, how can the space station, which is only about 200 miles (320 km) above Earth, have zero gravity? Read on to answer this and many other questions about gravity.

ARISTOTLE'S THEORY

The quest to understand gravity has been under way for a long time. Many of the ideas about it were conceived more than 2,000 years ago by the Greek natural philosopher Aristotle.

Figure 1.1   NASA flight engineer Nicole Stott participates in a space walk outside the International Space Station in September 2009.

No other theory of gravitation has survived, essentially un-changed, for as long as did Aristotle's. This is amazing because it could have been disproved much earlier with a simple experiment. Yet, because Aristotle's sway was so great, few philosophers were willing to dispute him. Aristotle held that everything on Earth had its natural place. Rocks, for instance, came from the earth, and because they wanted to be in their natural place, they fell to the ground. For the same reason, water flows downhill. Fire and air, however, want to be part of the sky, so they move upward.

Because downward motion was caused by an object's efforts to get to its natural place, Aristotle figured that the heavier the object, the faster it would move to reach its goal. This led to a key conclu-sion: Heavy objects fall faster than light ones. This universally ac-cepted postulate would confound scientists and stall scientific dis-covery for almost two millennia.

For some situations, this is a commonsense conclusion: Feathers do fall at a slower speed than rocks fall.

Yet why didn't some curious Greek simply break a brick in two and then drop one of those halves along with a whole brick from a height at the same time to see if the half brick fell slower than the whole one? This is hard to fathom. Historians believe that the

Teleology

Aristotle's thinking about nature was based on the philosophical concept called **teleology**. This approach to the natural world assumes that the processes of nature have a goal, or a purpose. Rocks really do "want" to be in the ground so they fall toward the earth. Fire wants to be in the heavens, so flames flare upward into the sky.

Although scientists would later disprove Aristotle's ideas about the causes of **motion**, teleological thinking did not end. In fact, it still persists. Modern ideas about purpose in nature have shifted from trying to understand the motion of inanimate objects to trying to understand how complex biological systems are constructed. Many people believe that the intricate, interacting parts of living creatures (especially human beings) could not have been formed by the directionless process of evolution by natural selection. They believe a designer, a God with a purpose, must have guided our construction (or creation).

A majority of Americans accept this teleological argument. However, most scientists reject it. In a 2007 survey by the Pew Research Center, David Masci wrote: "All but a small number of scientists regard Darwin's theory of evolution through natural selection as an established fact. And yet, a substantial majority of Americans, many of whom are deeply religious, reject the notion that life evolved through natural forces alone."

Aristotle's teleological laws of motion reigned supreme for two millennia. So, it is not surprising that his approach to science still lives on in the minds of many Americans.

early natural philosophers (as scientists and mathematicians were called) felt it was beneath their dignity, perhaps even an insult to their intelligence, to perform experiments. So, it should come as no surprise that the first dent in Aristotle's theory about the speed of falling objects came not from a laboratory but from a thought experiment.

In the sixteenth century, Giovanni Benedetti was born into a wealthy family in Venice. Studying alone and with tutors, which was not an uncommon practice then, he educated himself in mathematics and natural philosophy. What would happen, he asked, if two bodies joined by a thin weightless rod were dropped from a height? The answer was that because they are joined, the object would fall at a speed that was proportional to its total weight. Benedetti next wondered, what would happen if the rod were cut and the two bodies were dropped separately from the same height? Clearly, Benedetti concluded, the two would fall at the same rate as they did when were joined together. It seems likely, he concluded, that the speed at which objects fall is independent of how much they weigh.

Benedetti's thought experiment cast doubt on Aristotle's ideas, but his approach to the mechanics of falling bodies was almost as imprecise as Aristotle's. How fast do objects fall? And what, if not their weight, determines their speed? The man who would finally dismantle Aristotle's long-standing ideas about falling bodies was Galileo Galilei.

GALILEO GALILEI

Galileo was born in Pisa, Italy, in 1564. His father was a celebrated musician, but almost nothing is known about his mother. From his earliest days at the University of Pisa, Galileo was considered to be a smart, but pugnacious, sort. He argued with his professors, and one of his ongoing arguments was a dispute over Aristotelian science. Galileo doubted the great philosopher's claim that bodies fall at a rate proportional to their weight. To settle the argument, Galileo proposed an audacious plan: He decided to conduct an experiment to test Aristotle's theory.

Experiments were not the way one settled arguments in the late sixteenth century. Reason was preferred to data. Nevertheless,

Galileo proceeded with his test. The details of the experiment were not recorded. All historians know is that he dropped objects of differing weights from a tower, but whether they were cannonballs or other kinds of objects has been lost to history. Legend has it that the experiment was performed at the Leaning Tower of Pisa, but that, too, is not known for sure. In his last book, *Dialogues Concerning Two New Sciences*, Galileo has one character, Sagredo, describe the experiment: "But I . . . who have made the test can assure you that a cannon ball weighing one or two hundred pounds, or even more, will not reach the ground by as much as a span ahead of a musket ball weighing only half a pound, provided both are dropped from a height of 200 cubits."

Was Sagredo referring to Galileo's Leaning Tower test? Probably not. A cubit is approximately equal to 46 centimeters. Thus, a 200-cubit tower would be about 302 feet (92 meters) tall. The Leaning Tower, however, is less than 198 feet (60 m) tall. But why should it matter what height the objects were dropped from? Wherever Galileo conducted his test, he would have reached the same important conclusion: In the absence of air resistance, heavier objects fall at the same rate as lighter ones. This result was dramatically confirmed in 1971 by astronaut David Scott. Standing on the airless surface of the Moon, he simultaneously dropped a feather and a hammer. The two objects hit the ground at the same time. Unlike some television viewers, Galileo would not have been surprised.

Galileo's experiment overturned centuries of unquestioning acceptance of Aristotle's theory. It introduced the modern methods of science in which hypothesis is followed by testing. It also led Galileo to another question. It is clear that when an object is dropped, it starts with a velocity of zero and accelerates to a higher velocity. So, then, how fast do objects fall?

GALILEO'S PROBLEM

Galileo faced a big hurdle in trying to answer that question. The difficulty lies in the fact that objects fall so fast that it is hard to measure the very short amount of time that passes during the fall. Accurate time pieces were not available back in Galileo's day. And without some kind of clock, it is almost impossible to determine

Figure 1.2   In this illustration, Italian astronomer and physicist Galileo Galilei is seen using a telescope circa 1620.

the **acceleration** of a falling object. Somewhere around 1604, Galileo came up with a technique to slow the rate of an object's fall in order to measure its acceleration. Instead of dropping objects off a tower, it would be easier to measure their speed by rolling them down a ramp.

Unlike Galileo's tower test, historians do not have to guess how this experiment was performed. Galileo describes it in his *Dialogues Concerning Two New Sciences*:

> A piece of wooden moulding or scantling, about 12 cubits long [18 feet; 5.5 m], half a cubit wide [9 inches; 23 centimeters], and three finger-breadths thick, was taken; on

its edge was cut a channel a little more than one finger in breadth; having made this groove very straight, smooth, and polished, and having lined it with parchment, also as smooth and polished as possible, we rolled along it a hard, smooth, and very round bronze ball.

Before performing any experiments, Galileo had to make one assumption. "The speeds acquired by one and the same body moving down planes of different inclinations are equal when the heights of those planes are equal." In other words, if a person starts a "hard, smooth, and very round ball" (such as a marble) rolling down a plane (or ramp) with a height of, say, 3.3 feet (1 m), then the speed of the marble at the bottom of the ramp will always be the same, no matter

Figure 1.3   This painting depicts an inclined plane experiment Galileo is alleged to have made during his time as lecturer at Pisa. To the left and right are Prince Giovanni de Medici and Galileo's scientific opponents. These were influential men associated with various universities, and some are shown bending over the book of Aristotle, where it was written that, according to the rules of gravity, bodies of unequal weight fall with different speeds. Galileo (the tallest person in the picture, surrounded by a group of students) had boldly stated the opposite view. Physics showed him to be right.

the angle of the ramp. This means that the speed of a ball rolling down a ramp depends only on the height of the ramp. Furthermore, that speed will be exactly the same as that reached by a marble dropped vertically from the same height.

A Question of Terminology

In science, the words *speed* and *velocity* have different meanings. To add to the confusion, convention dictates that the symbol v is used for speed as well as for velocity. Thus, the formula for speed is usually shown as v = d/t, where d is the distance traveled and t is the elapsed time. This formula says that if a car goes 50 miles (80 km) in one hour, then its average speed is 50 miles per hour. Speed has no direction associated with it. Thus, the car might have averaged 50 miles per hour, but it did not necessarily go 50 miles from where it started. In fact, if the driver was running errands, the car might have ended up at its starting point. Quantities such as speed and temperature, where direction is either unnecessary or unspecified, are called **scalar quantities**.

The term *velocity* contains more information than *speed*. In the case of the car that went 50 miles, only the word *speed* makes any sense because no direction is stated. However, if the car traveled 50 miles due north, then one could say its average velocity was 50 miles per hour. Furthermore, the car must now be 50 miles north of where it started. Quantities with direction associated with them are called **vector quantities**. In vectors, both magnitude (50 miles per hour) and direction (due north) must be stated. Vectors are usually represented in boldface. Thus, one would write the equation for velocity (as opposed to speed) as

$$\mathbf{v}_{avg} = \mathbf{d}/t$$

This equation looks very much like the one for speed, except that the bold letters indicate that velocity (**v**) and distance (**d**) are vector quantities. Time, of course, is a scalar.

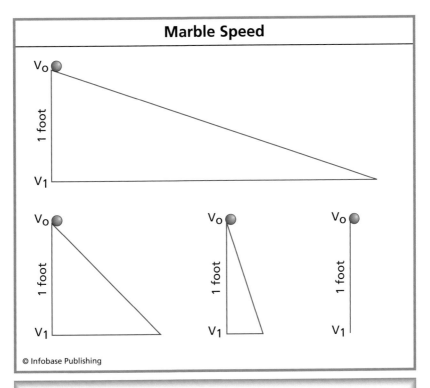

Figure 1.4 The final speed of the marble is the same for all experiments.

Of course, the marble rolling down the ramp would take longer to reach the bottom than one dropped from the same height. Yet its speed at the bottom would be the same. Galileo had figured out how to slow time for falling bodies. Now, he could begin to measure the acceleration of a body falling under the influence of gravity.

However, he still had the problem of accurately measuring time. Even if he could measure the time it took for the marble to roll the entire length of the ramp, that measurement would only give the average speed of the marble. As mentioned earlier, this can be stated mathematically as

$$v_{avg} = d/t$$

where v_{avg} is the average speed of the marble, d is the distance traveled on the ramp, and t is the time it took to reach the bottom.

To calculate acceleration, though, Galileo needed to know not the average speed of the marble but instead how that speed changes with time. The magnitude of the acceleration (a) is the change in speed with time. It is equal to the speed of the marble measured at a given time t_2 minus the speed at an earlier time t_1 divided by the time that passed between the two measurements.

$$a = (v_2 - v_1)/(t_2 - t_1)$$

Notice that if an object is gaining speed, that is if its speed at t_2 is greater than its speed at an earlier time, t_1, then the acceleration will be a positive number. If the object is slowing down, its acceleration will be negative. A negative acceleration is called a deceleration.

To find the acceleration of the marble as it rolled down the ramp, Galileo marked the distances on the ramp with regular points that were about 1 millimeter apart. Now, it was a simple task of letting the marble roll down the ramp and recording the number of marks it passed in a certain interval of time. To accomplish this, Galileo needed to be able to measure time accurately.

The times involved were very short. It only took only seconds for the ball to roll down the ramp. Galileo needed to measure the time it took for the ball to roll halfway down, a quarter-way down, and so forth. How did he do it? The answer is that no one knows for sure. Galileo's notes do not provide the answer. In fact, a few historians of science doubt that Galileo actually made any measurements at all. They suspect that he just made up some numbers to fit his preconceived hypothesis. However, science historian Stillman Drake, who thoroughly studied Galileo's experiment, came up with a better idea.

Drake knew that Galileo did not have to know the time. He just needed to divide time into equal segments and mark the position of the marble on the ramp at those times. So, Stillman says, what Galileo most likely did was attach adjustable frets to the ramp (like the raised bands on the neck of a guitar) that made a noise when the marble rolled over them. Galileo, the son of an eminent musician and pretty good lute player himself, could have easily adjusted the position of the frets until he produced a regular beat; that is, when an equal amount of time elapsed between each beat.

Because Galileo had already marked the ramp with regular points, it was now just a matter of recording the positions of the frets that gave the regular beat. Galileo's results are given below. Keep in mind that the times given are the number of frets that the marble has rolled over, and the distances between the frets are measured in the points that Galileo marked on his ramp. To come up with the crucial result, Galileo did not need to know the absolute values of either time or distance. Thus, the measures of times and distances in Table 1.1 are arbitrary, useful only in relation to other times and distances measured in the experiment.

Table 1.1 Galileo's Data						
Time	0	1	2	3	4	5
Distance	0	33	130	298	526	824

After centuries of speculation about the nature of gravity, someone had finally collected some data. It was not obvious, however, what the data were trying to tell Galileo, and he puzzled over them for some time. He manipulated the numbers this way and that as he attempted to make sense of the experiment.

He must have wondered, "What is the acceleration due to gravity?" The answer is that it is the rate of change of velocity of a falling object. So, how must the velocity of the marble rolling down an inclined plane change, if its acceleration was uniform; that is, if it gained speed at a constant rate? In other words, how far did the marble roll during time period 2 compared to time period 1?

Table 1.2 Distance Covered in Points for Each Time Interval	
Interval 1, t_0 to t_1	$33 - 0 = 33$
Interval 2, t_1 to t_2	$130 - 33 = 98$
Interval 3, t_2 to t_3	$298 - 130 = 168$
Interval 4, t_3 to t_4:	$526 - 298 = 228$
Interval 5, t_4 to t_5	$824 - 526 = 298$

To simplify these results, divide each number by 33. Then, calculate the distances at the end of each time period as shown in Table 1.3.

Table 1.3 Calculating Distances Covered		
Time (t)	Distances Covered for Each Time Period	Total Distance Covered at the End of Each Time Period
1	33/33=1.0	0 +1.0=1.0
2	98/33=3.0	1.0+3.0=4.0
3	168/33=5.1	4.0+5.1=9.1
4	228/33=6.9	9.1+6.9=16.0
5	298/33=9.0	16.0+9.0=25.0

A side-by-side comparison of the distance traveled by the marble at the end of each time period revealed the relationship for which Galileo was searching.

Table 1.4 Galileo's Breakthrough					
Time	1	2	3	4	5
Distance	1	4.0	9.1	16.0	25.5

Finally, it was clear to Galileo what the data were trying to tell him. Under the influence of gravity, bodies drop a distance that is proportional to the square of the length of time they have been falling. Drop a cannon ball or a musket ball from the Leaning Tower of Pisa (or any other tower). After 1 unit of time, the balls will have a dropped a distance proportional to $1^2 = 1$ unit of distance. After 2 units of time, they will have dropped $2^2 = 4$ units of distance. After 3 units of time, both balls will be $3^2 = 9$ units of distance below the point they were released. And so on. After x units of time, the balls will be x^2 units of distance from the top of the tower. (Keep in mind that the units used for time and distance will change the absolute value of these numbers but not the relationship between them. Also note that the tiny variations between the experimental data and the values one would calculate show just how good an experimenter Galileo was.)

For the first time in history, the relationship between time and distance for a free-falling body was known. It could be summed up in a single, simple equation:

$$d \propto t^2$$

In this equation, d is the distance the object has fallen, t is the time since it began its fall, and $\propto$ is the mathematical symbol for "proportional to." Notice that weight of the object plays no role in its rate of descent. Galileo had put Aristotle's long-running gravitational ideas to rest once and for all.

Galileo continued to do good science for the rest of his life. He developed elementary laws of motion, figured out the trajectories of cannonballs after they were shot, improved the telescope, and discovered that moons were orbiting Jupiter. His work in astronomy convinced him that Copernicus's view of the solar system—that Earth revolved around the Sun rather than vice-versa—was correct. This opinion got him into trouble with the Catholic Church. And in an often-told story, Galileo, under the threat of torture, was forced to recant his ideas about what revolved around what in the solar system.

Perhaps his troubles with the church sidetracked him, but Galileo never got around to expanding his work on gravity beyond Earth. He was unable to formulate a more general law, one that is not limited to our planet. He died—blind and under house arrest—at age 77 in 1642. Later in that same year came the birth of the man who would extend Galileo's ideas about gravity to encompass not just Earth but the entire universe. That man was Isaac Newton.

2

Newton to
the Rescue

Rolling marbles down planes and dropping balls from towers, leaning or not, helped Galileo study how bodies fall on the surface of the Earth. Like many learned men in those days, though, his bigger goal was to understand the heavens. Galileo and other scientists wanted to answer a question that had puzzled humankind since the first person gazed at the night sky: Why do the stars and planets move as they do? Galileo would take giant steps toward achieving that goal in 1609.

By then, he was a respected, 45-year-old scientist and teacher who had written two books. Still, he was supporting two sisters and a wandering minstrel brother who squandered money. Galileo was broke and in debt. He needed something to jump-start his career. That something was the telescope.

Even today, some people believe that Galileo invented the telescope. He did not, though he did substantially improve it. He was also quick to see that a tool that enabled one to identify distant objects would have enormous practical value. It would, Galileo figured, allow the leaders of Venice, an Italian seaport town, to spot invading enemy ships long before they actually arrived, thereby giving them a head start in preparing the city's defense. To impress the city's leaders, Galileo put on a well-orchestrated demonstration of the practical value of the telescope. Believing he had invented the device, a misapprehension Galileo did not correct, the grateful merchants of Venice doubled his salary.

Yet Galileo was more than just a newly well-to-do con man. He was a superb, committed scientist. So, while the gentry of Venice trained their telescopes on the seas, Galileo watched the skies. He looked first at the Moon, our nearest neighbor in space. Aristotle had written that the Moon was a perfect sphere, composed of a uniform, celestial material. Galileo disposed of that long-standing notion: The Moon, he wrote is "not robed in a smooth and polished surface," but is "... rough and uneven, covered everywhere, just like Earth's surface, with huge prominences, deep valleys, and chasms." Galileo's observations with the telescope made him one of the two best-known astronomers of his day. The other one was Johannes Kepler.

KEPLER ORDERS THE HEAVENS

Modern astronomy began in 1543 when Nicolaus Copernicus proposed a startling new theory. Earth, Copernicus proclaimed, revolved around the Sun rather than vice versa. This concept overturned centuries of Earth-centered dogma and led astronomy toward its first firm scientific footing. Copernicus's new system was simple. All the planets orbited the Sun in perfectly circular orbits. Although many astronomers laughed at these radical ideas, a few did not. And two of the most prominent believers in Copernicus's system were Galileo Galilei and Johannes Kepler.

Galileo and Kepler were contemporaries, but that was about all they had in common. Galileo was an argumentative, self-assured self-promoter. Kepler was poor and sickly, a neurotic mystic whose early scientific efforts were amateurish and arcane as he searched for some idealized version of the Universe where perfect, celestial spheres circled one another.

Yet Kepler was also a marvelously intuitive theorist whom philosopher Immanuel Kant—no mean theorist himself—called "the most acute thinker ever born." Kepler used his talents to extend the Copernican theory of the solar system and develop the laws that describe the motions of the planets. These laws, coupled with Galileo's

Figure 2.1 German mathematician and astronomer Johannes Kepler is best known for his laws of planetary motion, which provided the foundation for Isaac Newton's theory of universal gravitation.

insights about the motion of marbles rolling down ramps, would set the stage for the first scientific theory of gravity.

Kepler took the first steps toward his laws while working on the seemingly intractable problem of determining the orbit of Mars. When watched night after night, the planet would track a smooth course across the night skies, then stop and begin to move in the opposite direction. The Copernican system could not account for Mars's wandering ways.

We know how Kepler approached the problem. He fiddled around with the numbers, trying idea after idea (which is exactly what working scientists do today when faced with a mound of unexplained data). He tested circle after circle—in all 70 different circular orbits—but Mars stubbornly refused to follow any of the orbits he tested. Finally, he tried something different and discovered the solution. "I have the answer," he wrote to a friend. "The orbit of the planet is a perfect **ellipse.**"

Kepler soon figured out that the orbits of all the planets were elliptical. This discovery disturbed him. It went against his views of the solar system as some perfectly harmonious combination of circles and spheres. Thus, he kept searching for an underlying harmony. In the years that followed, he discovered the harmonies he was looking for. The result was **Kepler's three laws of planetary motion**, the first laws to order the heavens and make sense of what humans had been observing in the night skies for millennia.

These laws have been shown to be correct time and again in predicting the motion of the planets in the solar system. Yet they are more universal than even Kepler could have imagined. His laws have been used by astronomers to detect deviations in the motions of galaxies in **galaxy clusters** millions of **light years** away from the solar system.

As brilliant as Kepler was, though, he could only take his ideas so far. His laws were purely empirical. They accurately described the motions of heavenly bodies but had no theoretical foundation. Why do the planets follow elliptical orbits? Kepler had no answer.

Furthermore, he was unable to connect his laws to Galileo's discoveries in his work with ramps and marbles. Neither man had grasped the universal nature of gravity—that the same law that caused marbles to roll down a ramp also dictated the orbits of the planets.

Had the two men met, they might have gone further than simply ordering the heavens; they might have taken a crucial step toward understanding why the planets move as they do. But Galileo had just published *Starry Messenger*, a new best-selling book that described his discoveries with the telescope, and he was thoroughly enjoying his celebrity. So, he stiff-armed Kepler, who wrote him letters begging for one of his improved telescopes. As a result, the two men never got together. However, their work did pave the way for Isaac Newton, who made the connection that eluded both Kepler and Galileo.

A VERY IMPORTANT LUNCH

The publication of the first workable theory of gravity can be traced to a fashionable London coffee house where, in January 1684, three men gathered to sip bowls of coffee, eat lunch, and discuss the nature of gravity. They were Sir Christopher Wren, an established scientist and the architect of St. Paul's cathedral; Robert Hooke, a physicist and astronomer; and Edmond Halley, a well-regarded astronomer whose name would someday be given to a famous comet.

Properties of Ellipses

Kepler figured out that all the planets revolve around the Sun in elliptical orbits. To understand how gravity works in the solar system, one should know some of the features of this important geometric shape.

An ellipse is a squashed (or elongated) circle. Its eccentricity is a measure of how squashed or elongated it is. Two important features of an ellipse are its axes. The longest straight line across an ellipse is called its major axis, the shortest is the minor axis.

An ellipse is defined by two points called the foci (the plural of focus). The sum of the distance from the two foci to any point on the ellipse is a constant. An ellipse with only one focus would have major and minor axes of the same length, which makes it a circle. A circle has an eccentricity of zero, while a highly elongated ellipse has an eccentricity approaching one.

Earth's orbit is almost circular and therefore has a low eccentricity. The orbit of Mars, on the other hand, is more

They started their meeting by discussing the **inverse-square law**. This law had been around for centuries. It was formulated to explain the amount of light falling on an area of fixed size on the interior surface of a sphere if the source of the illumination is in the center of the sphere. (To illustrate, think of a light bulb located in the center of a basketball.) Because the surface area of a sphere increases with the square of the radius, the amount of light falling on area A must decrease as the square of the radius increases. This is easily shown.

The formula for calculating the surface area of a sphere is

$$\text{Area} = 4\pi r^2$$

In this formula, r is the radius of the sphere. Thus, for r = 1, the surface area of the sphere would be 4π. If r = 2, the surface area would be 16π, which is four times larger. Thus, the amount of light (or

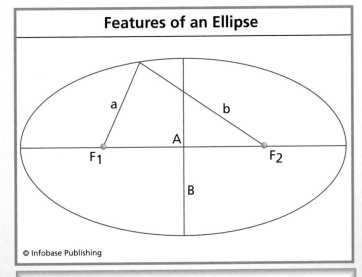

Features of an Ellipse

© Infobase Publishing

Figure 2.2 F_1 and F_2 are the foci of an ellipse with a major axis of length A and a minor axis of length B. At any point on the ellipse, a+b=constant.

eccentric, which accounts for the difficulty Kepler had in trying to cram its movements into a circle.

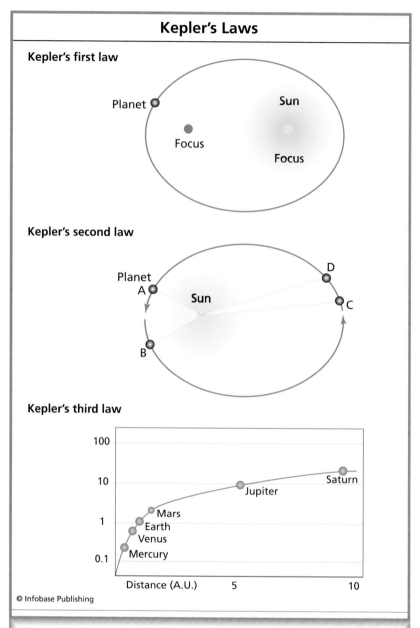

Figure 2.3 In Kepler's first law, the orbit of each planet is in the shape of an ellipse, with the Sun as one of its foci. In the second law, a planet sweeps out an equal area in equal time in its orbit around the Sun. Thus, time *AB*=time *CD* and area *ABSun*=*CDSun*. In the third law, the cube of the distance of each planet from the Sun is proportional to the square of its orbital period, so $P^2 \propto D^3$.

energy) from a source located in the center of the sphere falling on area of the sphere's surface must decline by a factor of 4 as r increases from 1 to 2. Similarly, for r = 3, the intensity of light falling on the area would be only $\frac{1}{9}$ as much as that on the sphere with r = 1.

Wren, Hooke, and Halley believed that this law could be applied to gravity. The attractive force between two objects should decrease with the square of the distance between them—just as the intensity of light did—as shown in the following:

$$F \propto 1/d^2$$

where F is the gravitational force between the objects, and d is the distance between them.

Wren, Hooke, and Halley suspected that some version of the inverse square law would lead to an improved understanding of gravity. That, in turn, might provide the theoretical foundation lacking in Kepler's laws of planetary motion. The discussion led

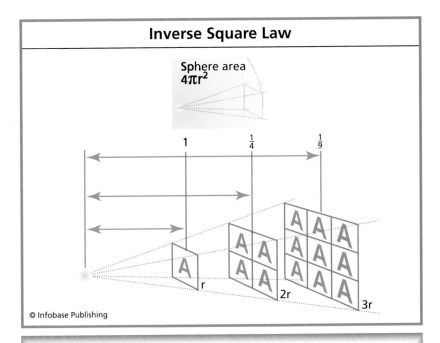

Figure 2.4   The inverse square law states that some physical quantity is inversely proportional to the square of the distance from the source of that physical quantity.

Wren to issue a challenge to his two friends. He would give a prize to the man who could demonstrate the mathematical connection between Kepler's laws and the inverse square law.

After two months, neither Hooke nor Halley had made much progress. Yet Halley knew of one person who just might be able to connect the two laws—a brilliant, testy loner named Isaac Newton who lived in Cambridge. Halley had met Newton once and decided to pay him a visit.

Halley asked Newton what path a planet would follow if the attraction between it and the Sun varied with the square of the distance between them. According to a close friend of Newton's, "Sir Isaac replied immediately that it would be an ellipsis."

Defining Distance

The distance between two objects seems a simple enough concept to need no further explanation. However, that is not the case. Consider the case of two iron balls sitting near one another. What is the distance between them? There are infinite possibilities, depending on where on the balls you measure from and to. Three of the simpler ways to measure the distance are illustrated (Figure 2.5).

The only distance that will give the correct gravitational attraction between the two balls is d_3, the distance between their center points. For any object, such a point is called its **center of mass**. It is the spot where the entire mass of an object can be said to be concentrated. The example here assumes that the mass of each ball is uniformly distributed. That is, its density is constant. This is a reasonable assumption for objects made of iron. But determining the center of mass for objects with nonuniform densities and with more complicated shapes—for example, a hammer with a wooden handle—is more difficult. It can be done, however, because every object has a center of mass. And the gravitational attraction between the two objects can be considered as acting between those centers.

This was the answer Halley hoped to hear. He asked Newton how he knew it. "I have calculated it," replied the sage of Cambridge. Newton then searched his papers for the calculations but could not find them. He then promised Halley he would redo the analysis and send it to him. What followed would drag on longer than expected and would try Halley's patience. Yet the result would prove to be well worth the frustration of dealing with the difficult Newton.

THE PRINCIPIA

It took Newton two years to arrange his thoughts, but arrange them he did. The end product of the London coffee-shop challenge was

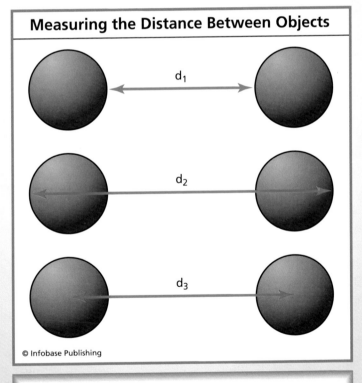

Figure 2.5   Three simple ways to measure distance between objects is shown.

the most important science book ever written and one of the most important books of any genre. It was called *Mathematical Principles of Natural Philosophy*—known today as *The Principia.* In it, Newton spelled out three laws of motion. He began by defining terms: mass, motion, and force. He followed this with three of the most basic laws of physics, now known as Newton's laws of motion.

1. Every body perseveres in its state of being at rest or of moving uniformly straight forward, except insofar as it is compelled to change its state by forces impressed.
2. A change in motion is proportional to the motive force impressed and takes place along the straight line in which that force is impressed. This law is usually stated as an equation: F = ma. Here, F is the applied force, m is the mass of the object, and a is the acceleration that the force imparts to it.
3. To any action there is always an opposite and equal re-action; in other words, the action of two bodies upon each other are always equal and always opposite in direction.

This is genius. People had been puzzling over how and why things moved for millennia. Galileo's insights had foreshadowed Newton's first law, but no one had even come close to getting at the entire truth about how forces interact with matter before Newton. Here were the answers to nature's most fundamental questions summarized in a few sentences.

In addition to being the most important science book ever written, *The Principia* is also one of the most difficult. Newton's methods were considered to be convoluted in the seventeenth century, and today, they are impossible for all but a few scholars to follow. In fact, Newton told a friend that he had deliberately made *The Principia* as unreadable as possible "to avoid being bated by little smatterers in mathematics."

Neither *The Principia* nor later interviews with Newton make it clear how he came up with his most famous law, the **law of universal gravitation**. There is, of course, the story about the young Newton sitting beneath an apple tree and wondering if the force that pulled the apple to the earth was the same force that held the Moon in its orbit.

Figure 2.6 Sir Isaac Newton's 1687 book *Philosophiae Naturalis Principia Mathematica*, better known as *The Principia*, describes in mathematical terms the principles of time, force, and motion that have guided the development of modern physical science. It stated the three fundamental laws of motion as well as the law of universal gravity.

Yet that story was probably invented; Newton himself said that he discovered the secrets of gravity "by thinking of them without ceasing." And that version seems to fit what we know about his workaholic habits better than the inspiration of the falling apple.

In any case, Newton developed a theory that explained not just *how* but *why* the planets move as they do. The theory also provided the mathematical foundation that enabled him to derive Kepler's laws. Those laws, so empirical and so accurate, now made sense because they revealed the force that dictated the motions of celestial objects. "It is now established," Newton wrote, "that this force is gravity. . . ."

The law quantifying this force is called Newton's law of universal gravitation. It states that every object in the universe is attracted to every other object. The force of attraction between any two of them is proportional to the masses of the objects and inversely proportional to the square of the distance between them. This statement can be summarized in a famous equation:

$$F \propto m_1 m_2 / d^2$$

Or as it is more commonly written:

$$F = G m_1 m_2 / d^2$$

where G is the gravitational constant, which has the same value everywhere in the universe. This important constant is often called the "Big G."

The Principia catapulted Newton to rock-star fame, despite the fact that few people could understand it. His laws of motion and his concept of universal gravitation awed scientists of that era. But Newton's impact went far beyond the scientific world. His work led to the French Age of Enlightenment and changed forever the way much of mankind views the world. The physical world does not follow the rules of capricious gods or kings; it follows the laws of science, the laws of Newton.

Newton died in 1727 at the age of 84. He was buried with honor in Westminster Abbey, where he lies alongside England's most famous politicians, poets, kings, and philosophers. Alexander Pope wrote an epitaph summarizing Newton's contributions: "Nature and Nature's laws lay hid in night; God said, 'Let Newton be!' and all was light."

APPLYING NEWTON'S LAW

The unsung hero of *The Principia* was Edmond Halley. First, he encouraged Newton to write it, which meant dealing regularly with the difficult author. Next, although he was not a rich man, Halley financed its publication. Finally, he used Newton's laws to predict a spectacular event. The event was the periodic appearance of the comet that now bears his name.

The Royal Society

All of the participants in the fateful 1684 lunch that stimulated Newton's writing of *The Principia* were Fellows (as members are called) of the Royal Society. England's oldest scientific group began in 1660 with 12 men, one of whom was Christopher Wren, the man who convened the lunch. Robert Hooke was the first Curator of Experiments, and Edmond Halley was a young up-and-coming member.

The man who would solve the problem discussed at the lunch was also a member. Isaac Newton had been invited to join the Royal Society in 1672, years before *The Principia* propelled him to fame and fortune. Later, the Fellows elected him president.

Shortly after its founding, the Society began publishing books and research papers. Its scientific journal, *Philosophical Transactions*, first issued in 1665, is still being published today, making it the longest-running scientific journal in the world. The Society's motto has also remained unchanged: *Nullius in verba*, which means "take nobody's word for it."

Today, the Society's original membership of 12 has grown to about 1,400. In 1945, women were finally allowed to join the Fellows. And time has in no way diminished the Society's prestige. The initials FRS (Fellow of the Royal Society) behind the name of a scientist carry as much weight today as they did when Newton was running the show.

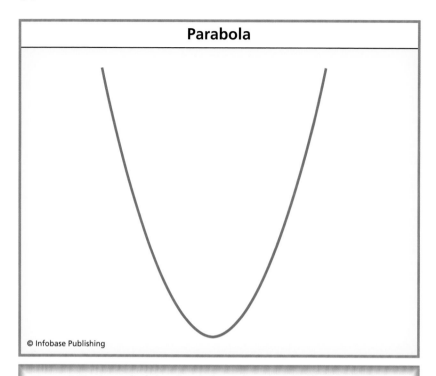

Parabola

© Infobase Publishing

Figure 2.7 A parabola is a bowl-shaped curve. Isaac Newton was among a number of astronomers who initially believed that all comets followed a parabolic orbit, which is the path followed by some objects that pass near a massive body. Comets in parabolic orbits are deflected by the Sun's gravity but are one-time events, shooting off into space after they pass the Sun never to return.

Although closely associated with Newton, Halley did more than cling to the great man's coattails. He was an outstanding scientist in his own right. He was born in 1656 in Shoreditch, an area in London likely named for a sewer that once flowed through it. Halley was already an accomplished astronomer and mathematician when he entered Oxford at age 17. Five years later, he was elected a Fellow of the Royal Society, becoming the youngest member of that august group.

Newton and most other astronomers believed that comets followed a **parabolic orbit**. If they were right, then a comet would appear just once, bending around the Sun then shooting off into space. Thus, every comet sighted would be a one-time event. Yet

Halley suspected that some comets traced out ellipses, a possibility predicted by Newton's law of gravitation. Also, he figured, if some comets traveled in elliptical orbits, then the same comet would reappear periodically, orbiting the Sun just as the planets do.

Halley studied the paths of comets as recorded by generations of sky watchers. One of them in particular seemed to follow an elliptical path. It had appeared in 1682, but Halley believed that the same comet had previously brightened the night sky in 1531 and 1607. After some calculations, he predicted the comet would return in 1758, 76 years after its last sighting. Halley knew he would not be alive to see it as he would have been more than 100 years old by then. But return it did, right on schedule, and it was named for the man who predicted its appearance.

Halley had a long and productive career in science. He composed the first meteorological chart and developed mortality tables, creating the mathematical basis for life insurance. Nowadays, these accomplishments, and even his contribution toward getting Newton's masterpiece published, are pretty much forgotten. Still, Halley's name lives on in his comet. Every 76 or so years, he is celebrated by those who know little about the man and his outstanding career in science. But they do recognize the glowing trail left by that ball of rocks and ice streaking through the night sky.

3

Using Newton's Law

The famous equation of universal gravitation attributed to Newton is found in every physics textbook:

$$F = Gm_1m_2/d^2$$

The equation is not, however, found anywhere in *The Principia*. Newton never expressed the law in this form. He preferred the proportionality expression:

$$F \propto m_1m_2/d^2$$

To convert Newton's proportionality to today's familiar equation, one must make the two sides equal to one another by inserting the **proportionality constant** G. Newton had no idea of the value of G. To calculate it, one must measure the force of attraction between two objects of known mass. The first person to perform this experiment had, like Newton, little interest in the constant G itself. His name was Henry Cavendish, and his goal was to weigh Earth.

THE CAVENDISH EXPERIMENT

Make no mistake about it: Some scientists are strange. Yet there is no reason to think they are any more unconventional than men and women in other lines of work. Poets and politicians can act strangely,

Figure 3.1 British scientist Henry Cavendish performed an experiment in 1797-1798 to measure the force of gravity between masses in a laboratory. He used this result to accurately determine the mass of Earth.

too. Yet, perhaps due the persistent popularity of Dr. Frankenstein and his monster, the stereotype of the mad scientist lives on in the modern mind. Henry Cavendish was no Dr. Frankenstein, but he definitely fit the eccentric-scientist mold.

Cavendish was born in 1731. Although his birthplace was in France, he spent most of his life in London. He was the scion of one of England's most prominent families and was rumored to be the richest man in the realm. His life's focus was science, and his research was first class. One biographer called him "the wisest of the rich and the richest of the wise." And he was possibly the oddest character in either category.

Another biographer characterized Cavendish as having a "most reserved disposition, bordering on disease." He was, in fact, pathologically shy, especially with women. In one often-told story, he is said to have added a staircase in his house for the housekeepers so he could avoid encountering them.

Except for meetings of the Royal Society, Henry Cavendish had no social life. As a consequence, he left no personal correspondence. George Wilson, a writer who labored long and hard to produce a biography of Cavendish, dug deeply into his subject's psyche, searching for an inner core. Cavendish was, he finally concluded, a "man without a heart."

This assessment seems overly harsh. Today, someone like Cavendish might be diagnosed as mildly autistic or suffering from Asperger's syndrome. In any case, Cavendish's peculiar habits and personality did not stand in the way of his doing good science. He is recognized as the person who discovered hydrogen. He was also the first person to show that water was a **compound** not an **element**. And, in one of the most difficult and sensitive experiments ever performed, Henry Cavendish measured the density of Earth.

Today, many physics textbooks state that Cavendish was the first man to measure the gravitational constant. He was not. Using the results of his experiment, Cavendish could have calculated the Big G, something that even Newton had not accomplished. But he had no interest in it. His mind was fixed on what he regarded as a more pressing problem.

By the middle of the eighteenth century, geologists had accurately determined the size of Earth. The next question was, how much did it weigh? To figure this out, scientists needed to know its mean density. This was a crucial piece of information for astronomers. If they knew Earth's density, they could calculate the densities of the Moon and the planets in the solar system. Scientists of the day trekked all over the world trying various techniques to estimate the density of the planet. All of these methods were indirect and included assumptions that were open to question.

Finally, one scientist, John Michell, devised a special balance that he thought would settle the density issue. Unfortunately, he

The Other Cavendish

The Cavendish Laboratory at Cambridge University was founded in 1874, and, from its earliest days, has played a prominent role in British science. Its first director was the distinguished Scottish physicist James Clerk Maxwell, the man who united electricity and magnetism. Later directors included J.J. Thomson and Ernest Rutherford, the Nobel laureates who played key roles in determining the structure of atoms. The Cavendish (as it is called) has been and still is one of the premier physics research labs in the world. So, it is natural to assume that Henry Cavendish, one of England's great scientists—and one who was wealthy enough to build a research lab out of pocket change—funded it. Yet, as it turns out, he did not.

Before the Cavendish came into existence, most science labs were housed in private homes or in college rooms. Newton's lab was in his rooms at Trinity College. Henry Cavendish's was in his house. In the nineteenth century, it became clear that universities needed their own labs for research and to train students. Cambridge responded by creating a committee that recommended appointing a professor and "giving him a demonstrator, a lecture-room, a laboratory, and several class-rooms, with a sufficient stock of apparatus."

Unfortunately, the university was short of funds at the time, so the plan did not go forward. A year or so later, William Cavendish, the chancellor of the university and a distant relative of Henry Cavendish, made an extraordinarily generous offer. He put up the substantial sum of money needed to build the lab. The lab was later named for the Cavendish family, to commemorate the benevolent academic and the great scientist.

died before he could experiment with it. He was, however, one of Henry Cavendish's few friends, and Cavendish decided to undertake the experiment Michell had planned.

The special balance Michell designed is called a torsion balance. This is a device that measures the force required to twist a wire or fiber. Michell (and Cavendish) wanted to use the balance to measure the attractive force exerted by gravity between lead balls. To minimize air currents, Cavendish enclosed the balance in a wooden box. Each of the two large balls weighed 348 pounds (158 kilograms) (Figure 3.2). The small ones, which were attached to the arm of the balance, tipped the scales at 1.6 pounds (0.73 kg).

Cavendish knew the experiment he had in mind would be a difficult one. He stated the problem succinctly: "As the force with which the balls are attracted . . . is excessively minute, not more than 1/50,000,000 of their weight, it is plain that a very minute disturbing force will be sufficient to destroy the success of the experiment."

The details of Cavendish's famous experiment are complicated and unnecessary for our purposes. The end result was a measurement of the attractive force between the large and small balls. By comparing the measured force between the balls to the force of Earth's gravity on the smaller ball, Cavendish came up with the mean density of Earth. Our planet was, he calculated, 5.48 times as dense as water. Considering the extreme sensitivity of the apparatus and the many possibilities for experimental error, this result is uncannily close to today's accepted value of 5.52.

Surprisingly, no one bothered to use the Cavendish experiment to calculate G for almost a hundred years. In 1892, the British physicist C.V. Boys calculated G using Cavendish's data. The result (in today's **SI units**) was 6.75×10^{-11} $m^3kg^{-1}s^{-2}$, again very close to the currently accepted value of 6.67×10^{-11} $m^3kg^{-1}s^{-2}$.

At its most fundamental level, though, Cavendish's accomplishment was not providing the data to calculate the Big G. Nor was it his determination of the density and mass of Earth. No, Cavendish's contribution went deeper. He was the first person to demonstrate experimentally that ordinary objects attract one another. Scientists now knew that Newton's law of gravitation was truly universal. And they would use that knowledge to make a prediction about the solar system that was even more dramatic than the reappearance of Halley's comet.

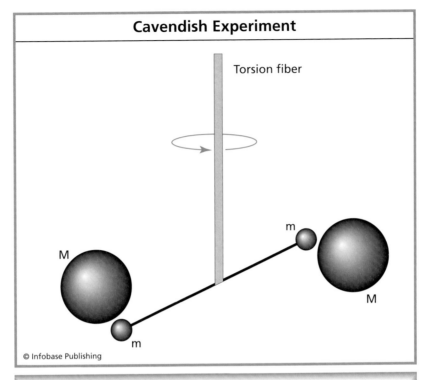

Cavendish Experiment

Torsion fiber

m

M

M

m

© Infobase Publishing

Figure 3.2 In the Cavendish experiment, Henry Cavendish used a torsion balance apparatus, based on one developed years earlier by geologist John Michell, to make a series of measurements. His goal was to measure the weight of Earth.

A NEW PLANET?

In the middle of the eighteenth century, most learned people knew that exactly six planets circled our Sun—Mercury, Venus, Earth, Mars, Saturn, and Jupiter. They were certain about this because they could see five of these planets with the naked eye from the planet they were standing on, Earth. However, this view of the solar system changed in 1781 when astronomers using telescopes spied a seventh planet, which was later named Uranus.

For a while, nothing much changed. Astronomers, scanning the skies with the best telescopes of the day, discovered no new planets. However, their observations did reveal that the new planet acted oddly. It was not following a proper orbit around the Sun, the orbit predicted by Newton's law of gravitation.

Alexis Bouvard, a French astronomer, was the first to identify the problem. In 1821, he reviewed all the observations of Uranus and reached a confounding conclusion. Sometimes Uranus moved faster than predicted. At other times it moved slower. Could Newton's law of universal gravitation be wrong? Or was something disturbing Uranus's orbit?

Almost 25 years later, two mathematicians working independently tackled the problem: Frenchman Jean Joseph Le Verrier and John Couch Adams, a young Englishman. Both men believed that Newton was right, and, using his laws of motion and gravity, they predicted the existence of a new planet. Even today, science historians argue about which of the two men predicted the new planet's position first and then actually saw it. (Until recently, the consensus was to award the honor to both men, but newly discovered documents have led some historians to give full credit for the discovery to Le Verrier.)

In any case, in 1845 or 1846 (depending on which account one accepts), astronomers trained their telescopes on the area where the calculations predicted the mysterious body that was altering the orbit of Uranus should be found. They soon spotted a new planet that was later named Neptune. The new planet's orbit was outside that of Uranus. And its gravitational attraction could both retard and increase the speed of Uranus, depending on the position of the planets relative to one another (Figure 3.3).

This spectacular find confirmed Newton's laws. With no more than pen, paper, and Newton's laws, astronomers had found a new planet.

THE (WEAK) FORCE OF GRAVITY

Gravity dominates the universe. The force of gravity changed the orbit of Uranus and pointed the way to Neptune. It also holds Earth, the Sun, and the Milky Way together. It keeps us humans firmly planted on the surface of our planet. It also keeps our planet from following the straight line predicted by Newton's first law of motion and zooming off into space. These facts make it easy to conclude that gravity

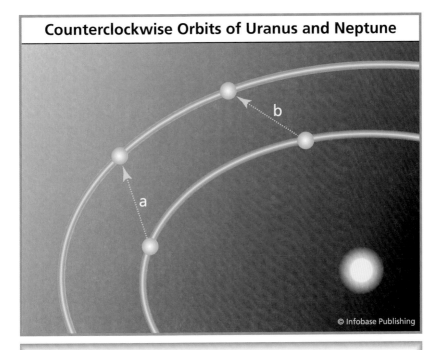

Counterclockwise Orbits of Uranus and Neptune

b

a

© Infobase Publishing

Figure 3.3   At position a, the outer planet (Neptune) pulls the inner planet (Uranus) ahead of its predicted position. At position b, Neptune retards the motion of Uranus.

is a strong force. However, such a conclusion turns out to be wrong. Gravity is actually a very weak force.

As usual, the best way to test such an assertion is to do an experiment or a calculation. In this case, a calculation will do. Let's use Newton's equation to determine the force of attraction between two massive lead balls, each weighing 2,205 pounds (1,000 kg), when their centers of mass are separated by about 3.3 feet (1 meter).

$$F = Gm_1m_2/d^2$$
$$F = (G)(10^6)\ kg^2/1m^2$$
$$F = (6.67 \times 10^{-11}\ m^3\ kg^{-1}\ s^{-2})(10^6\ kg^2\ m^{-2})$$
$$F = 6.67 \times 10^{-5}\ m\ kg\ s^{-2}$$

or

$$F = 6.67 \times 10^{-5}\ N$$

Here, F is the attractive force between the balls, and N is the symbol for the newton, the SI unit of force. One newton is the force required to accelerate an at-rest object with a mass of one kilogram to a speed of one meter per second in one second. In the **gravitational field** at Earth's surface, one newton equals 0.102 kilogram force (a 1 kilogram force is the force exerted by a 1 kilogram mass in the gravitational field at Earth's surface). Thus, the attractive force between two 1,000 kilogram weights can be expressed as

$$F = (6.67 \times 10^{-5} \text{ N})(0.102 \text{ kgf/N})$$
$$F = 6.81 \times 10^{-6} \text{ kgf}$$

or

$$F = 6.81 \times 10^{-3} \text{ gram force (gf)}$$

Thus, the gravitational force between the two balls, each weighing more than a ton, amounts to only 0.0067 gram-force or 0.00024 ounce-force. This is an "excessively minute" force, just as Henry Cavendish predicted. Of course, the attractive force increases as the balls are moved closer to one another. Still, even if they were nearly touching, only 1 centimeter (about 0.4 inches) apart, the gravitational force between two balls would be the equivalent of less than 0.1 gram (0.003 ounces).

These calculations demonstrate how weak the force of gravity is. The **electrostatic force** between charged objects is trillions of times stronger. Still, gravity does dominate the universe —and our planet. Someone falling just a short distance can be injured, and a fall from a great height can be fatal, as hundreds of suicidal jumpers have proved. The reason this wimpy force plays such a big part in our lives is because we live in close proximity to a really massive object, namely planet Earth. Henry Cavendish himself calculated that the mass of Earth is 6×10^{24} kilograms, which is massive enough to exert a strong pull, even on lightweights such as us humans. And that is why jumping off tall bridges (or buildings or cliffs) is hazardous to one's health.

The Mystery
of the Tides

Humans have puzzled over the tides for almost as long as they have wondered about the movement of the planets in the night sky. Newton showed that both phenomena are driven by the same force: gravity. Yet long before Newton, the Greeks were speculating that the tides were related to the heavens, especially to the lunar cycle. By 55 B.C., one Greek philosopher had noted that "the movement of the ocean is subject to periods like those of the heavenly bodies . . . behaving in accord with the Moon."

Of course, more fanciful theories were also offered. In his 2007 book, *Ebb and Flow*, Tom Koppel recounts the views of one early geographer ". . . the Moon warmed the bottom of the sea, which drew water out from the Earth; that water expanded in volume and made [the] sea level rise." By the time of the Renaissance, though, such tales were pretty much discounted. Most learned people thought that the tides and the Moon were directly linked.

Still, not all of them believed in that link. Galileo Galilei, the greatest scientist in the era before Newton, was a hard-nosed experimentalist. He disagreed with the notion that two bodies separated in space could so dramatically affect one another.

The tides, Galileo speculated, arose from the absolute motion of the Earth. The combination of the Earth's rotation and its orbit around the Sun means that the part of the planet that is away from the Sun moves faster than the part closest to the Sun. This differential acceleration acting on a large body of water would cause it to slosh around just as a pail of water sloshes around when it spins. Furthermore, because of Earth's rotation on its own axis, the positions of maximum and minimum speed would change every 24 hours. The net result would be the tides.

Galileo's model had a big flaw: It predicted that the Earth would experience one high and one low tide per day. However, most seashores experience two tides a day. Galileo tried to explain away this objection to no avail. Finally, even he began to doubt the hypothesis. "I hope," he wrote, "that this idea does not turn out to be delusive, like a dream which gives a brief image of truth followed by an immediate certainty of falsity."

In most of his endeavors, Galileo got the science right. However, his explanation of the source of the tides was way off the mark. His error may have stemmed from his firm belief in the Copernican system. Galileo accepted that Earth was spinning on its own axis and orbiting the Sun. And, like most good scientists, he was willing to go out on a limb for a risky idea in which he believed. Also, like most good scientists, he was willing to admit to the possibility of being wrong.

NEWTON'S BETTER IDEA

Along most coasts, the high and low tides occur about an hour later every day. If high tide rolls in at noon today, it will come in at about one o'clock tomorrow afternoon. The Moon has the same built-in, one-hour lag; it rises about an hour later than the night before. Surely, there must be some relationship between these two events. Yet the nature of that relationship remained hidden until Newton proposed his law of universal gravitation.

If all masses attract all other masses, as Newton's law states, then the oceans should be attracted by Earth's nearest neighbor, the Moon. The first man to apply this law to the tides was Isaac Newton himself. Imagine, as he did, an Earth that is completely covered with water. Now, consider a simple system composed of just Earth and the Moon. The side of Earth nearest to the Moon will experience a gravitational pull toward it, creating a watery bulge (Figure 4.1).

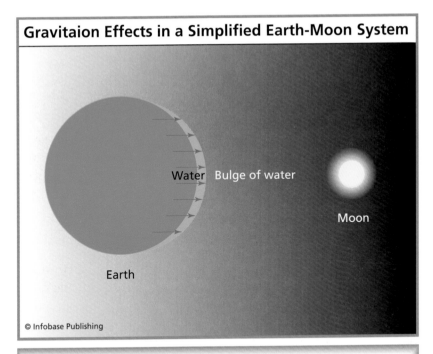

Gravitaion Effects in a Simplified Earth-Moon System

Water   Bulge of water

Moon

Earth

© Infobase Publishing

Figure 4.1   This simplified drawing of the Earth-Moon system shows how gravitational properties affect the Earth. The bulge denotes the distortion of water in response to the combined gravitational effects of the Moon and the Sun.

As Earth rotates, the position of the bulge relative to the Moon never changes. But the position of the bulge on Earth does. Visualize this by imagining an island in the sea. Let's call it Atlantis and represent it with the letter A as shown in Figure 4.2. In this simple model, although Earth and the Moon are at rest relative to one another, Earth's rotation causes Atlantis and every other spot on Earth to experience one high and one low tide every 24 hours.

It is easy to spot the problem with this model. It is the same one that scuttled Galileo's idea. Most coastlines experience not the one high tide per day as predicted by this model but two high tides. Even a simple model must account for the **semidiurnal** (meaning twice a day) flow of the tides.

The real Earth-Moon system creates two tidal cycles a day because a watery bulge also forms on the side of Earth away from the

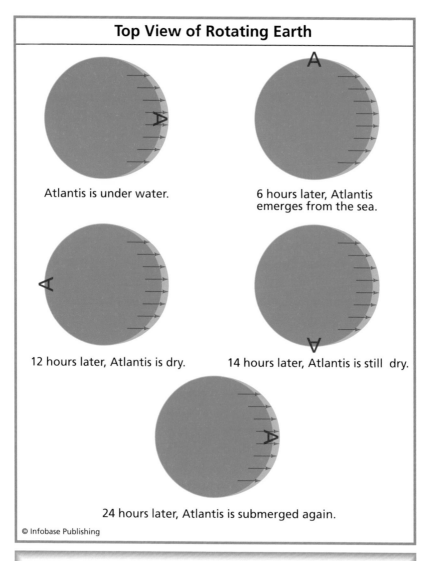

Top View of Rotating Earth

Atlantis is under water.

6 hours later, Atlantis emerges from the sea.

12 hours later, Atlantis is dry.

14 hours later, Atlantis is still dry.

24 hours later, Atlantis is submerged again.

© Infobase Publishing

Figure 4.2 This simplified drawing shows how gravitational pull affects the Earth as it rotates over time.

Moon, as shown in Figure 4.3. This means that Earth has two bulges that are opposite one another. Both bulges are stationary relative to the Moon. But the planet revolves beneath them, producing two high tides every 24 hours, submerging the unfortunate residents of Atlantis twice a day.

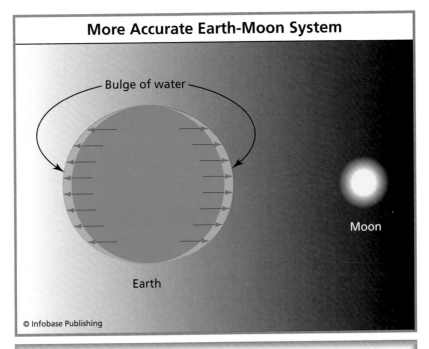

More Accurate Earth-Moon System

Bulge of water

Moon

Earth

© Infobase Publishing

Figure 4.3 In reality, the Earth-Moon system produces two bulges because Earth and the Moon do not appear the same—or have the same relational effects—at every point on Earth.

Two bulges arise because the gravitational forces between Moon and Earth are not the same at every point on Earth. Earth's near side is closer to the Moon than its far side. This results in a gravitational force that is 7% stronger on the near side. The variation in the gravitational forces acting on Earth stretches it along the Earth-Moonline and compresses it along the north-south axis. The result is the net tidal forces shown in Figure 4.4.

Without getting into a lot of complicated mathematics, it is hard to understand how gravity produces two bulges on opposite sides of Earth. However, there is a simple, if imprecise, way to think about it. The near bulge is due to the higher gravitational attraction of the water closest to the Moon. The far bulge forms because that side of Earth is farther from the Moon, and the gravitational attraction is weaker. The result is two bulges—and two high and low tides a day.

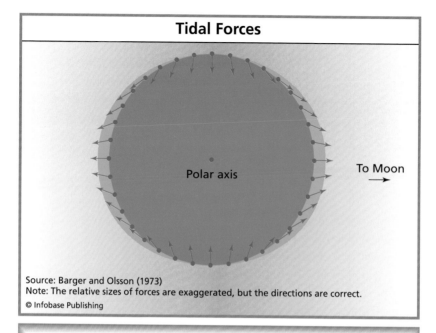

Tidal Forces

Polar axis

To Moon

Source: Barger and Olsson (1973)
Note: The relative sizes of forces are exaggerated, but the directions are correct.
© Infobase Publishing

Figure 4.4 Gravity produces tidal forces. Because the gravitational force exerted on one body by a second body is not constant across its diameter, bulges form on the sides nearest to and farthest from the second body.

A COMPLICATION

The model presented above neglects an important fact. Not all tides at a given location have the same magnitude. Exceptionally high and low tides occur periodically. Unusually high tides are called **spring tides**, even though they have nothing to do with that season. Very low tides are known as **neap tides**. Our crude model does not account for these tidal extremes because the largest object in the solar system is missing from it. A more complete picture of the gravitational forces affecting Earth must include the Sun.

Although the Sun is much more massive than the Moon, it is farther from Earth. So, the tidal force exerted by the Sun is only about half that of the Moon. However, its effect is still substantial. As a consequence, to understand the tides, one must take into account not only the positions of Earth and the Moon, but also the position of the Sun.

Spring tides rise when the Sun and the Moon are aligned (Figure 4.5b and 4.5c). It is no surprise that when the Sun and the Moon are on the same side of Earth (Figure 4.5b), that the tides are higher than normal. In this case, both the Sun and the Moon are pulling on the water creating a bigger bulge than usual. However, the bulge is also exaggerated when the Sun and the Moon are on opposite sides of the planet.

To see why, refer back to Figure 4.4. The Sun has a similar tide-generating effect as the Moon, differing only in magnitude. And because the Sun and the Moon are exactly opposite one another

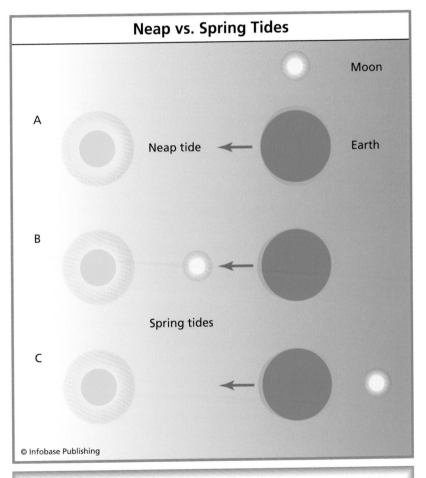

© Infobase Publishing

Figure 4.5   High and low tides occur because of the alignment of the Sun, the Moon, and Earth.

relative to Earth, the two effects reinforce each other and create larger-than-normal water bulges (Figure 4.5). The result is two unusually high tides a day at the seashore.

Neap tides occur when the Sun and the Moon are at right angles to each other relative to Earth (Figure 4.5a). In this case, the gravitational fields of the Sun and the Moon interfere with one another, reducing the tide-generating force. The result is high tides that are lower than normal and low tides that are higher. The tidal range, the difference in height between high and low tides, is about 10% to 30% smaller than normal during a neap tide.

MORE COMPLICATIONS

By now, a careful reader may have noticed quite a few weasel words — such as *usually* and *almost*. The lack of certainty stems from the first simple assumption in our model, namely an Earth that is entirely covered with water. Of course, the planet we live on is not—and that complicates the situation.

To start with, Earth's continents break up the smooth ocean described in the model. Furthermore, the depths of the oceans vary, and peninsulas and islands impede the flow of the water; in addition, there are many other variables that affect the tides. The result of this real-world messiness is a substantial irregularity in how water moves around Earth. The tides along the coasts of eastern North America and northern Europe are primarily semidiurnal—Cape Cod, Massachusetts, is a good example. Yet along the southern coast of the United States, in Mobile, Alabama, for instance, the tides are diurnal, with only one high and one low tide a day. A third category of tides is known as mixed tides. Mixed tides are a combination of the diurnal and semidiurnal and are usually characterized by two unequal high tides and two unequal low tides a day. The southern part of Western Australia experiences another mixed tidal pattern, consisting of both semidiurnal and diurnal cycles.

The magnitude of the tides also depends on the local geography. The huge tidal range in Nova Scotia's Bay of Fundy, for instance, is due in part to the fact that the bay is shaped like a funnel, which greatly amplifies the tides. Meanwhile, tides in the Caribbean and

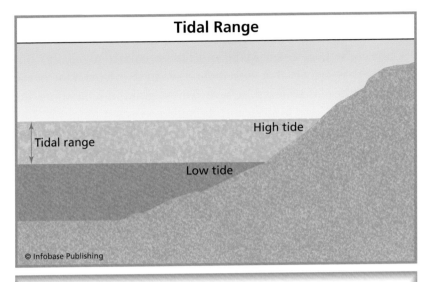

Figure 4.6   Tidal range is the height difference between high tide and low tide. The most extreme ranges occur around the times of new or full moons when the gravitational forces of the Sun and the Moon are acting in the same direction (new moon) or exactly the opposite way (full moon).

the Gulf of Mexico are more muted, with a range of less than 2 feet (0.6 m) at many beaches and harbors.

HARNESSING THE TIDES

Oceanic tides demonstrate the power of gravity to move water. The drive for clean, renewable energy has led several countries to investigate using this moving water as a source of energy. It is a good idea but not a new one. Humans have harnessed the tides for their own purposes for centuries.

A few hundred years ago, tide mills were located in suitable spots throughout coastal Europe and America. The principle behind them is simple. A dam with a sluice and a one-way gate is built across a tidal river or stream. The rising tide fills a reservoir on the upstream side of the dam. The gate closes when the tide begins to ebb. As the tide falls, the water stored behind the dam is released to turn a water wheel.

The earliest documented tide mill has been dated to A.D. 787, but archeologists suspect that even older mills have existed. One of the earliest of these is believed to have ground grain in London during Roman times. Some American tide mills go back a long way, too. One, in Hampton, New Hampshire, was approved for construction at a meeting on October 13, 1681. The river rights were awarded to two men who agreed to "build [the tide mill] and keep it in good order for the grinding of the town's corn; and that they make convenient gates to let out the water, that the flow not [change] any man's hay in hay-time . . ."

Instead of being used to grind corn, modern tide mills are used to generate electricity. The engineering approaches fall into two

A Most Unusual Race

Five Islands is a town on the coast of Nova Scotia, Canada. Once a year, it hosts a 5K and 10K race around the islands for which the town is named. The islands lie just offshore, rising precipitously from the deep waters surrounding them. You would normally assume that this race, like most water races, is a contest between power boats or sailing craft, kayaks or canoes, or maybe swimmers. But it is not. The clue to how this race is run can be found in its name—"Not Since Moses." This refers to how, in the Old Testament, Moses parted the waters and allowed the Israelites to cross the Red Sea on foot. The name fits here because this competition is run as a foot race around the islands.

Five Islands is on the shore of the Bay of Fundy, the home of the world's biggest tides. Twice a day, 100 billion tons of water flow into and out of the bay. The water can rise as much as 50 feet (15.2 m) from low tide to high tide. And at a very low tide, much of the water is sucked out of the bay, exposing the sea floor and permitting the running of a foot race, albeit a muddy one, around the islands.

main categories: barrage and tidal stream systems. A barrage is a barrier placed across a tidal river or stream. They work much like the old tide mills, trapping water behind the barrage at high tide and releasing it as the tide goes out. The out-flowing water turns the turbines, which generate electricity.

Barrages are expensive to build and may harm marine life. Consequently, only a few commercial installations are operating today. One of them, as you might guess, is located on the Bay of Fundy whose enormous tidal range makes it perfect for such an installation.

Tidal stream systems use the **kinetic energy** of moving water to power turbines directly. This technology relies on individual turbines placed in fast-flowing tidal waters. These systems act like underwater windmills. As the tide flows in or out, the moving water

Figure 4.7 This image shows a typical low tide near a dock in Canada's Bay of Fundy.

Probably no other event better showcases the extremes of the tides—and the power of gravity.

Figure 4.8 A seventeenth century tide mill sits beside the River Deben at Woodbridge in Suffolk, England. This type of water mill is driven by the rise and fall of the tides.

turns a turbine that generates electricity. These systems cost less to install, but they are costly to maintain. Furthermore, if they are not sited and managed properly, they can harm fish and water birds who are caught in the turbine's blades.

Because the tides ebb and flow regularly with the Moon and Sun, tidal power is more reliable than wind or solar power. The disadvantages lie primarily in its steep initial cost, high operating expense, and potential to do ecological damage. Nevertheless, several pilot-plant tests of tidal power are underway. If successful, then one day such appliances as air conditioners and furnaces may be powered by gravity.

SOMETHING FOR NOTHING?

Tidal power is a seemingly inexhaustible source of energy. Gravity powers the tides. And the supply of gravity is unlimited. This reasoning implies that the tides, which we can tap into for our own energy needs, will continue forever. But if that is so, then the Earth-Moon system is violating one of the most basic laws of science: the **conservation of energy**. This law says that energy can neither be created nor destroyed. Thus, the total amount of energy in a **closed system** is constant. As far as the tides are concerned, Earth and the Moon approximate a closed system. (The Sun, of course, plays a role, but let us ignore that for the moment.) So, if the tides are generating energy, something else in the system must be losing it, or else the law is wrong.

For centuries, quacks, charlatans, and even some solid citizens, have tried to get around the energy conservation law. One common approach is the perpetual motion machine, a device that runs forever with no added energy. Some of the ideas for such a machine are very clever and creative. Yet scientists have found a fallacy in every one of these machines. And this something-for-nothing story of the tides contains a fallacy, too.

Tidal friction arises from the movement of Earth beneath the tidal bulges. As the planet rotates, friction drags the bulge. Because Earth rotates faster than the Moon moves in its orbit, the bulge closest to the Moon actually does not point directly at it but leads it (Figure 4.9). As a consequence, the Moon is pulling back on the bulge, acting as a brake on Earth's rotation. Among other effects, this pull is slowing the planet's rotation. This means that the Earth is losing rotational kinetic energy. And this is the energy tradeoff: The energy the tides gain is balanced by the kinetic energy Earth

Werewolves and Vampires

The Moon and the tides have been the inspiration for some fanciful ideas—from machines that can run forever to legendary creatures such as werewolves. The full Moon seems to especially stimulate the imagination. People supposedly get a little crazy when the Moon is full. In fact, the word "lunatic" comes from Luna, the Roman goddess of the Moon. During medieval times, some Europeans believed that moonstruck humans could change into werewolves or vampires. Even today, some people maintain that a full Moon increases the number of fist fights, suicides, accidents, and other unpleasant events. Is there any truth to these claims?

Two psychology professors, Scott Lilienfeld and Hal Arkowitz, examined the issues in an article in *Scientific American Mind*. They wanted to find out if the higher gravitational forces experienced during a full Moon might produce violent (or bizarre) behavior. This is a far-fetched notion but not a totally ridiculous one. After all, the action of the tides prove that gravity can move water around. Because the human body is 80% water, it is possible that we might be affected by the added gravitational pull during a full moon.

Nonsense, the authors say. The pull of the Moon's gravity on a person is tiny, less than the force exerted by a mosquito perched on one's arm. Furthermore, the Moon's gravitational effect is just as great during a new moon, but no stories are told of vampires and werewolves emerging during those dark nights.

To cement their conclusions, the authors refer to a huge study that attempted to relate all sorts of events to periods of the full Moon. No relationship exists, the study's authors concluded. The belief that an unusually high number of strange events occur at the time of a full Moon is only "the perception of an association that does not exist." Once again, scientific analysis has debunked a folk tale. Next thing you know, scientists will be telling us that ghosts do not hang around haunted houses.

loses. The law of conservation of energy holds. You really cannot get something for nothing.

This slowing of Earth's rotation means that the next century will begin with a day that is 2 milliseconds longer that the one that began this century. In a few billion years, Earth's rotation will have slowed to the point that the days will be twice as long. The tides will be less frequent and less vigorous. As time passes, the tides will continue to diminish—eventually approaching zero.

Still, the conservation law tells us that energy cannot just vanish. So, where does that lost tidal energy go? The answer lies in the friction that slows Earth's rotation. Like any other brake, it generates heat. Heat is infrared radiation, another form of energy, much of which radiates into space.

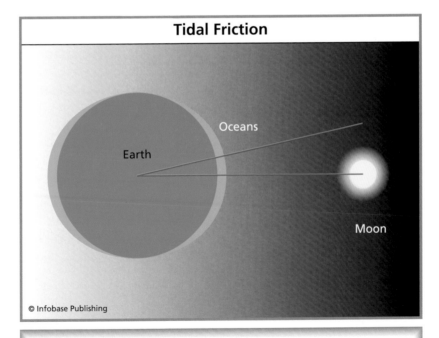

Figure 4.9   Tidal friction is a force between the oceans and the ocean floor caused by the gravitational attraction of the Moon. Over long periods of time, tidal friction decreases Earth's rate of spin, which lengthens the days. In turn, the Moon gains angular momentum in its orbit and gradually spirals away from Earth.

THE FORGOTTEN FACE OF THE MOON

The tidal forces that make the oceans bulge operate on the dry land, too. The solid Earth itself experiences a tidal cycle. Because rocks do not stretch as easily as water, the size of the bulge is smaller, about one-third the size of the one-meter water bulge found in mid-ocean. Nevertheless, these land bulges can have big effects.

Just as the Moon slows Earth's rotation, so Earth has slowed the Moon's. The Moon once rotated much faster on its own axis. Despite the fact that the Moon has no ocean, the same tidal forces that are slowing Earth's rotation were at work on the Moon. Yet Earth is much more massive than the Moon. Consequently, the effect of Earth's gravity on the Moon is more pronounced. It is so pronounced, in fact, that the Moon's rotation has slowed to the point that it no longer rotates relative to Earth. In this state, the Moon's tidal bulge is always aligned with the tidal force. This does not mean that the Moon is not rotating. It is. Yet the length of time it takes for one rotation is exactly the same as the time it takes to complete one orbit around Earth. This gravitational stalemate is called a **tidal lock**. And it is why the Moon presents only one face toward Earth.

EINSTEIN STEPS IN

Newton's formulation of the law of gravitational attraction explained so many astronomical and earthly events that by the beginning of the twentieth century, few scientists doubted the theory. But one scientist saw it more clearly than others and realized that although Newton's laws were correct under most circumstances, they did not hold true in certain conditions.

The scientist who had this brilliant insight was Albert Einstein, and his theory of relativity would show that Newton's law of universal gravitation was a special case of a broader law. Relativity also answered a question that Newton raised but was unable to answer: How can gravity act through a distance on two bodies that are not in contact with one another?

A Better Idea

The first person to identify a problem with Newton's law of gravitational attraction was Newton himself. How can the Sun, which never touches Earth, hold the planet in orbit around itself? How can its gravity reach out across 93 million miles of empty space and affect the trajectory of Earth? This action-at-a-distance property of gravity disturbed Newton. "I have not as yet been able," he wrote in *The Principia*, "to deduce from phenomena the reason for these properties of gravity, and I do not feign hypotheses."

More than two centuries would pass before someone did "feign hypotheses" to explain how gravity operates as it does. That person was Albert Einstein. His theory of relativity supplanted the Newtonian concepts of space, time, and gravity. Although Newton's famous inverse-square formula still works well for most applications, Einstein's approach would prove to be superior in extreme conditions where Newton's law fails.

Einstein's breakthrough came shortly after the beginning of the twentieth century, but a key component of his theory originated much earlier with the grandfather of modern physics, Galileo Galilei.

RELATIVE MOTION

"Motion," Galileo wrote in 1629, ". . . exists relatively to things that lack it; and among things which all share equally in any motion, it

Figure 5.1 German physicist Albert Einstein's early work on the theory of relativity (circa 1905) dealt only with systems or observers in uniform motion with respect to one another and is referred to as the special theory of relativity. In 1911, he noted the effects of gravitation on inertia. Four years later, he completed his mathematical formulation of a general theory of relativity. It stated that gravity was the result of the curvature of space-time. This curvature, he concluded, was due to the presence of objects with Mars.

does not act, and is as if it did not exist." In other words, motion exists only relative to other things. This concept was a key to understanding gravity.

No complicated experiments are needed to test Galileo's idea about the relativity of motion. Everyday experience confirms it. Consider an airplane with the shades pulled so the passengers cannot see out. If the air is smooth, there is no way for them to know that they are zooming along at a steady 500 miles per hour (805 km/hr) relative to Earth. Within the cabin of the plane it is, as Galileo said centuries earlier, as if the motion of the plane "did not exist."

Yet what happens to the laws of physics in the airplane? How would they compare to the laws determined by a physicist working in a lab on Earth? Galileo figured this out, too. Of course, he could not use an airplane to illustrate his answer, so he used a ship. In a famous passage in his book *Dialogue Concerning the Two Chief World Systems*, Galileo invites the reader to "Shut yourself up with some friend in the main cabin below decks on some large ship. . . ." He asks the reader to bring along (among other things) a few butterflies, a small bowl of water with fish in it, and a bottle that drips into a bowl beneath it. Watch what happens to the cargo when the ship is at rest: The butterflies flit about, the fish swim, and the bottle of water drips into the bowl beneath it. Now, have the ship proceed in any direction at a constant speed. "You will discover," Galileo writes, "not the least change in all the effects named, nor could you tell from any of them whether the ship was moving or standing still." The laws of physics, Galileo concluded, are the same for any observers moving in a straight line at a constant velocity.

This means that a juggler on Galileo's ship or in an airplane could juggle balls in the same way a juggler on solid ground would. Furthermore, if any physicists happened to be aboard the plane, any experiments they performed would obey the same laws that govern physics experiments carried out on Earth. And the laws would be identical to those determined by a scientist performing experiments in a rocket ship streaking away from Earth in a straight line at a constant 100,000 miles per hour (161,000 km/hr).

Of course, airplanes and rocket ships traveling at constant velocity are not stationary to an observer on Earth. They are moving. The motion that an observer (or instrument) detects depends on one's **frame of reference**. A frame of reference is simply your immediate surroundings, things that are participating in the same motion you are. Passengers who are seated in the cabin of an airplane are in the plane's frame of reference, and unless they look out a window, the plane seems motionless to them. Yet to an observer in a different frame of reference—say, looking up from Earth at the plane as it flies by—the plane is moving at 500 miles (805 kilometers) per hour. The point is that both of these representations of reality are equally valid and depend only on the reference frame chosen.

This conclusion leads to a central tenet of relativity: If two or more reference frames are in uniform motion, that is moving in a straight line with constant velocity and not rotating, then the laws of physics will be the same in all of those frames. Objects at rest will stay at rest and objects in uniform motion will remain in uniform motion, unless acted on by a force. Such frames are called **inertial reference frames**. With this definition in mind, the relativity tenet can be restated: In all inertial frames, the laws of physics are the same. It makes no difference if you are in an airplane, a rocket ship, or in a lab on Earth's surface, any physics experiment you carry out in any inertial frame—including juggling—will give the same results.

Let's rethink this: A reference frame attached to Earth—a physics lab for example—cannot be inertial, nor can a lab attached to the Sun. After all, Earth is not moving in a straight line. It is spinning on its own axis while orbiting the Sun. Furthermore, at the same time, the Sun is whirling around the Milky Way. How can Earth be an inertial reference frame?

In fact, it is not an inertial frame—at least not exactly. However, the effects due to Earth's rotational velocity are tiny to the point of being negligible, and the effects due to its orbit around the Sun are even smaller. Consequently, for most experiments, Earth acts as an inertial frame of reference, even when precision is crucial—as it would be in, say, sword juggling.

By now, the two main postulates that underpin relativity theory should be clear:

- Absolute motion does not exist. Objects move only in relation to other objects.
- Any physics experiment carried out entirely within an inertial frame of reference will give exactly the same result in any other inertial reference frame.

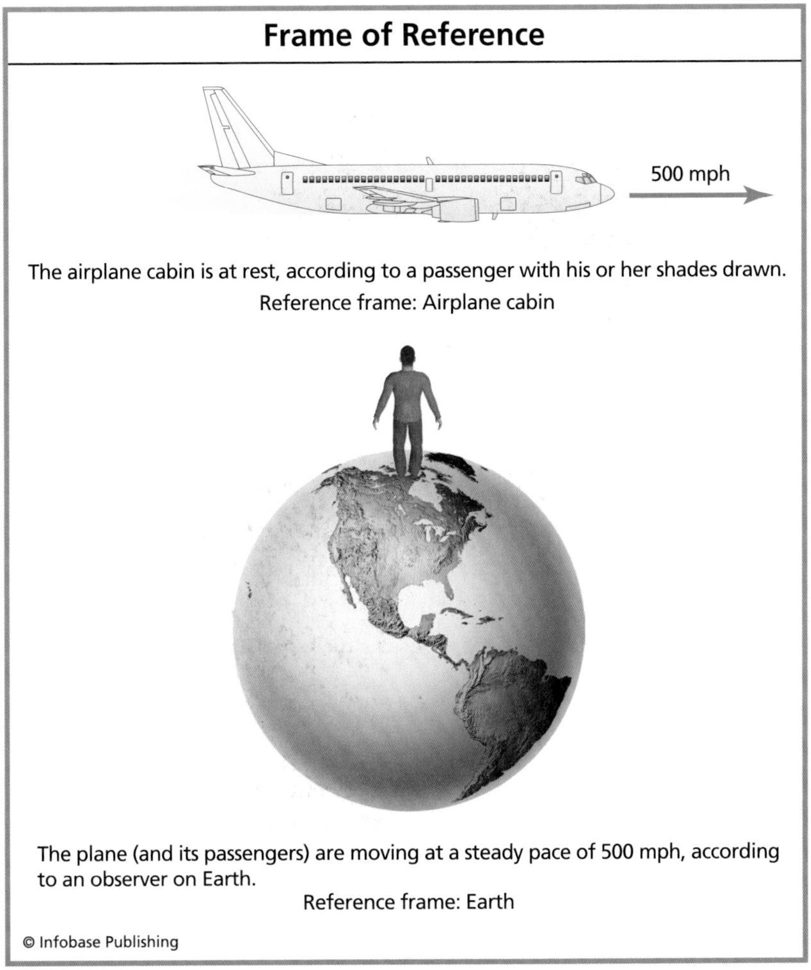

Frame of Reference

500 mph

The airplane cabin is at rest, according to a passenger with his or her shades drawn.
Reference frame: Airplane cabin

The plane (and its passengers) are moving at a steady pace of 500 mph, according to an observer on Earth.
Reference frame: Earth

© Infobase Publishing

Figure 5.2 A person's frame of reference determines how they see and experience things. The theory of special relativity predicts that time and distance depend on the frame of reference in which they are measured.

These two postulates—the relativity of motion and the unchanging laws of physics in inertial reference frames—are known today as Galilean relativity, in honor of the man who proposed them first.

Galileo's conclusions about motion lead to an obvious question: Is everything relative? The answer is no. Scottish physicist James Clerk Maxwell dispelled that notion in 1862.

Maxwell is celebrated today by a geeky T-shirt that displays four daunting equations on the front. These equations, derived by Maxwell, predict the existence of a special type of wave, now called an **electromagnetic wave**. Using his equations, Maxwell calculated the speed of electromagnetic waves and found that they traveled at the speed of light. This led him to the startling and important conclusion that light itself is a form of electromagnetic radiation.

EINSTEIN'S BIG IDEA

Maxwell's insight led to one of the most important questions facing scientists in the last half of the nineteenth century. If all motion is relative, as Galileo stated, then what is the speed of light relative to? Experiment after experiment gave the same result. The speed of light was always the same. Finally, Einstein reached an important conclusion. In a brilliant paper, his first on relativity, he wrote, "Light always propagates in empty space with a definite velocity v that is independent of the state of motion of the emitting body."

Einstein had long before accepted the relativity principle as laid down by Galileo. That is, for observers in all inertial reference frames, the laws of physics are the same. Because he believed Maxwell's equations expressed a fundamental law of physics, then light must travel at the same speed in all reference frames in uniform motion. This seemingly simple postulate leads to amazing consequences: Time, for instance, is not what it seems to be, and neither is space.

Let's begin with a simple thought experiment (Figure 5.4). Consider a box 186,000 miles (300,000 km) tall. Install a light flash emitter and a detector at the bottom of the box and a mirror at the top. Pump out the air. Activate the flash, and an observer, let's call her Alison (who is standing in the vacuum, holding her breath), measures the elapsed time. Because the speed of light in a vacuum is about 300,000 kilometers per second, two seconds will pass between emission and detection.

Now, look at the same box and the same two events from the perspective of another observer, who is named Darren. He is

Figure 5.3 Scottish physicist James Clerk Maxwell developed a set of equations—called Maxwell's equations—that united electricity and magnetism and predicted the existance of waves now called electromagnetic waves.

standing outside the box. The light box is moving in a straight line with velocity v relative to Darren. At t = 0, the flash goes off. The light beam hits the mirror and returns to the detector at t = t_1. This is the same light box, the same flash, the same two events as shown in the first part of Figure 5.4. However, from Darren's perspective, the light beam travels farther than it did from Alison's point of view. Recall Einstein's conclusion that the speed of light is the same in all uniformly moving reference frames. Because the light must travel farther in Darren's frame of reference, more time must elapse between flash and detection for Darren than it does for Alison.

This leads to a disconcerting conclusion. The elapsed time between the two events depends on the reference frame of the observer. This stretching of time is called **time dilation**. This effect is a property of time itself and is independent of the clock used to measure it. Try the same experiment using an atomic clock or your wrist watch. The result will be the same. "Moving clocks run slower" is the phrase often used to remember which clock measures the longer time between events. Alison—who is in the reference frame where the events take place—will always measure a shorter time than Darren. Furthermore, there is no "correct" time. Both measurements of the elapsed time are equally valid. Time is not absolute. It depends on your frame of reference.

One can show that space is relative, too. A spaceship heading for a distant star at close to the speed of light will measure a distance to the star that is less than the distance as measured from Earth. This effect is called **length contraction**. Space, like time, depends on one's frame of reference.

A MORE GENERAL THEORY

When Einstein published this work, he confined his ideas to the special case of reference frames moving in a straight line at constant velocity. Consequently, he called it the **special theory of relativity**. The **general theory of relativity**, which applies to all frames of reference, took Einstein ten more years to work out. It took so long because it included an entirely new concept of gravity.

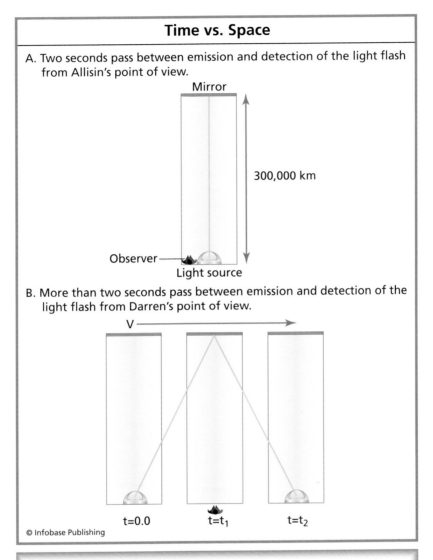

Time vs. Space

A. Two seconds pass between emission and detection of the light flash from Allisin's point of view.

Mirror

300,000 km

Observer

Light source

B. More than two seconds pass between emission and detection of the light flash from Darren's point of view.

V

t=0.0   t=t₁   t=t₂

© Infobase Publishing

Figure 5.4   The elapsed time between two events depends on the reference frame of the observer.

The first steps toward the general theory came from Einstein's former math professor, Hermann Minkowski. Minkowski was amazed that Einstein could come up with a scientific idea as elegant as the special theory. "It came as a tremendous surprise," he told another physicist, "for in his student days Einstein had been a lazy dog."

The special theory showed that time and space were relative. The time between two events varied depending on the reference frame in which it is measured. So, too, did the distance (or space) between events. How, then, could one specify when and where an event occurred?

To answer the question, Minkowski introduced a new concept, **space-time** or, as it is sometimes called, Minkowski space. By specifying the coordinates of an event in four-dimensional space-time, one could pinpoint where and when it took place. Three of these coordinates are the ordinary dimensions of space (x, y, and z). The fourth is time. One needs all four coordinates (x, y, z, and t) to pin down an event.

A Very Famous Experiment

The speed of sound in air is about 340 meters per second. Based on Galileo's hypothesis that all motion is relative, one should specify that its speed is relative to the molecules in the air through which the sound wave is passing. Sound waves cannot propagate through a vacuum. The transmission of sound requires a medium.

Earlier experiments by Thomas Young had established that light, like sound, was a wave. (Einstein would later show that under some conditions light can act as a particle.) Yet as the stars prove every night, light can travel though empty space. By the middle of the nineteenth century, its speed had been measured to be 300,000 kilometers per second. (Today, the accepted speed of light in a vacuum is 299,792 kilometers per second or 186,282 miles per second, which we will round off to 300,000 kilometers per second and 186,000 miles per second.) So, a big question facing physicists in the last half of the nineteenth century was what is that speed relative to?

Space-time is impossible for most of us visualize. The mathematics of it are also difficult to master. But the concept itself is simple enough. Minkowski himself summarized it somewhat dramatically: "Henceforth space by itself, and time by itself, are doomed to fade away into mere shadows, and only a union of the two will preserve an independent reality." Minkowski's insight was helpful to Einstein as he went about the grueling work of extending the special theory of relativity to reference frames not in uniform motion.

Einstein realized that the problem with special relativity lies in the sneaky term "uniform motion." How do you know when you are not in uniform motion? Usually, it is an easy question. If you are in a car turning a corner or accelerating, you will feel it. You will be pushed to the side or pressed into the car seat. When an airplane

The prime candidate for the medium through which electromagnetic radiation propagated was a substance called the **luminiferous ether**. The ether was assumed to be everywhere, but exactly what it was remained a mystery. In 1887, two scientists—Albert Michelson and Edward Morley—attacked the problem with an experiment that aimed to directly detect the ether. The experiment, arguably the most famous in all of science, is now universally referred to as the Michelson-Morley experiment.

Carrying out the experiment was a difficult and delicate task. The entire apparatus used in the experiment was floated in a pool of mercury to minimize the effects of vibration. The results, which were checked and double-checked, shocked the experimenters and the scientific community. No ether could be detected. No matter how the apparatus was set up, the speed of light never changed.

It is not known whether or not this result helped Einstein formulate his theory of relativity. Yet its conclusions—that there is no ether, and the speed of light in a vacuum is always 300,000 kilometer per second—cleared the air for the work of future scientists.

encounters nonuniform motion in the form of turbulent weather, drinks are spilled and pretzels fly all over the cabin. Things that are easy to do in uniform-motion reference frames, such as juggling, are almost impossible in frames of nonuniform motion.

More About Time Dilation

Time was a fixed quantity to Isaac Newton. It was the same throughout the universe. "Absolute . . . time," he wrote, "in and of itself and of its own nature, without reference to anything external, flows uniformly . . ." Einstein showed clearly that Newton was wrong. Absolute time does not exist. Time is relative. It depends on the reference frame in which it is measured, as demonstrated in the thought experiment with the light box. But how could Newton be wrong? His concepts of space and time have been and continue to be applied to all sorts of problems, and they consistently give the right answers. A simple calculation, again involving Alison and Darren, will shed light on this mystery.

Using the Pythagorean theorem and a little algebra, an equation can be derived that relates the elapsed time of an event as measured by two observers in inertial reference frames moving with respect to one another.

$$t_A = t_B \sqrt{1 - \frac{v^2}{c^2}}$$

In this equation, t_A is the time elapsed between emission and detection of the light beam as measured by Alison, who is in the box's frame of reference, and t_B is the elapsed time as measured by Darren. As usual, the letter c represents the speed of light in a vacuum, and v is the velocity of the light box moving relative to Darren.

Suppose Darren is standing beside a highway. Traffic is moving from left to right at a steady 60 miles per hour (97 km/hr). Off goes the light flash. We know that Alison will measure a time from flash to detection of exactly two

Yet Einstein came up with a clever thought experiment in which uniform and nonuniform reference frames are indistinguishable. Consider a person enclosed in an elevator deep in outer space where gravitational effects are vanishingly small. What would happen if a

seconds. Using the previous equation, one can calculate how much time Darren would measure. Sixty miles per hour is 0.017 miles per second, so filling in the numbers gives us:

$$t_B = \frac{t_A}{\sqrt{1 - \dfrac{v^2}{c^2}}}$$

$$t_B = \frac{2}{\sqrt{1 - \dfrac{(0.0166)^2}{(186,000)^2}}}$$

$$t_B = \frac{2}{\sqrt{1 - \dfrac{0.00028}{(1.86 \times 10^5)^2}}} = \frac{2}{\sqrt{1 - \dfrac{2.8 \times 10^{-4}}{3.46 \times 10^{10}}}}$$

$$t_B = \frac{2}{\sqrt{1 - 0.81 \times 10^{-14}}}$$

Because 0.81×10^{-14} is vanishingly small, $t_B = 2$ seconds

The calculation shows that the difference between the two measured times is negligibly small. Even if Allison was moving at 100,000 miles per hour, the measured times would be essentially identical. And if she speeded up to an incredible 60,000,000 miles per hour, Darren would still measure a time of only 2.01 seconds, a mere 1/100th of a second more than Alison. Only as the relative velocity of the reference frames approaches the speed of light will Alison and Darren begin to measure significantly different elapsed times. So, for inertial reference frames that move at ordinary speeds relative to one another, relativistic effects can be ignored. In those cases, Newton's laws work just as well as Einstein's.

rocket accelerated the elevator upward at a rate of 32 feet (9.8 meters) per second? That is the same acceleration rate one experiences on the surface of Earth, the acceleration due to gravity. The passenger would feel her feet press on the floor of the elevator just as if she were standing on Earth. Furthermore, if she took a quarter from her purse and dropped it, the coin would fall to the floor just as it would on Earth. In fact, she could juggle swords if she chose to or perform any physics experiment. The results would be the same as if she were standing on Earth (Figure 5.5).

Is there any way the passenger in an enclosed room like an elevator could learn whether she is in Earth's gravitational field or in an accelerating reference frame? The answer, Einstein concluded, is no. Gravity is equivalent in every way to an accelerating reference frame. This **principle of equivalence** became a cornerstone of Einstein's general theory of relativity.

One consequence of this principle, Einstein realized, was its effect on light. When a flashlight is shined through a small hole in an enclosed room located deep in outer space, the beam goes straight across the room (Figure 5.6a). Now, let's attach a rocket to the floor of the room and ignite it. As it accelerates upward, the beam of light enters the hole but by the time it crosses the room, the room itself has moved upward. As a result, the light strikes the opposite wall at a point closer to the floor (Figure 5.6b).

The beam of light in the accelerating reference frame is no longer straight. It is bent. Yet the equivalence principle states that an accelerating reference frame is indistinguishable from a gravitational field. Thus, Einstein reasoned, gravity must bend light. Einstein would later use this startling conclusion to devise an experiment that would help substantiate his general theory of relativity.

WHAT IS GRAVITY?

After working on general relativity off and on for years, Einstein's ideas finally crystallized. Minkowski's work on the special theory showed that four-dimensional space-time was necessary to pinpoint events. And the principle of equivalence linked accelerating frames of reference to gravity. Yet Einstein needed to develop the

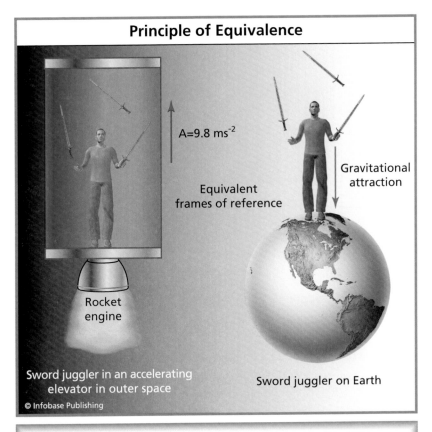

Principle of Equivalence

A=9.8 ms^{-2}

Equivalent
frames of reference

Gravitational
attraction

Rocket
engine

Sword juggler in an accelerating
elevator in outer space

Sword juggler on Earth

© Infobase Publishing

Figure 5.5   Gravity is equivalent in every way to an accelerating
reference frame.

mathematics to describe how matter in a gravitational field moves
through space-time.

In 1912, he began to work on the mathematics needed to express
the geometry of a four-dimensional universe. For centuries, the only
geometry available came from the Greek geometer Euclid, whose
textbook on the subject, *Elements*, is the best-selling mathematics
text ever written.

Euclidian geometry is the geometry taught in high school. It
tells us that parallel lines never intersect, and that the sum of the
angles in a triangle is always 180 degrees. Unfortunately, almost all
of these good, commonsense rules do not hold in the gravitational

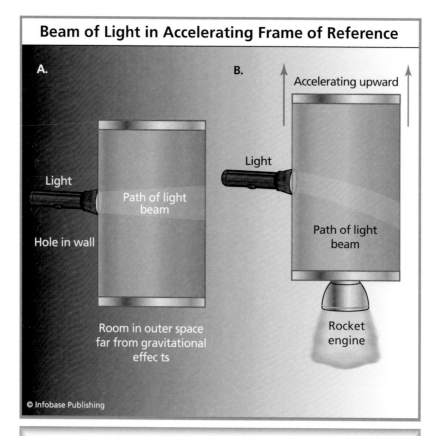

Beam of Light in Accelerating Frame of Reference

A.

Light

Path of light beam

Hole in wall

Room in outer space far from gravitational effec ts

B.

Accelerating upward

Light

Path of light beam

Rocket engine

© Infobase Publishing

Figure 5.6 This illustration highlights the theory of how gravity bends light.

fields of four-dimensional space-time. That left Einstein with a problem.

The equivalence principle told him that light followed a curved path in a gravitational field. Maybe, he speculated, space-time itself was curved. He needed a new geometry, one that predicted how objects would move in curved space-time.

Fortunately, such a geometry existed. A friend introduced him to the geometry of multidimensional spaces developed more than 50 years earlier by the German mathematician Bernhard Riemann. Riemann had developed mathematical methods to describe the curvature of space, including four-dimensional space. After much study, Einstein mastered the difficult math needed to represent a curved four-dimensional space.

Yet where did gravity fit in this four-dimensional curved universe? In one of the truly great leaps of imagination, Einstein "realized that the foundations of geometry have physical significance." In other words, gravity is curved space-time. Bending light beams are not really bending at all, they are following a straight line in curved space-time. What causes space-time to curve? Here, Einstein and Newton agree. Mass is responsible for gravity. However, the two men's concept of how it operates was entirely different.

Newton's first law states that acceleration requires a force. Yet Einstein realized that Newton's theory is not true in a gravitational field. Mass curves space-time in a manner that causes a body to accelerate with no forces acting on it. In a gravitational field, a body will follow the curvature of space-time toward another massive body. Finally, the action-at-a-distance question that puzzled Newton could be answered. Gravity is the curvature of space-time, which manifests itself as the attractive force between masses.

These are difficult ideas to get one's mind around. The mathematics are difficult, too. However, Einstein's complicated equations can be boiled down to a single concise and elegant mathematical description of space-time.

$$R_{\mu v} - \tfrac{1}{2} R \, g_{\mu v} = 8 \, \pi \, G \, T_{\mu v}$$

One can extract the essence of this equation without worrying about the precise meaning of the symbols, some of which are complex geometrical entities called **tensors**. As written, the left side of the equation describes the curved geometry of space. The right side specifies how matter moves in space-time. The equation looks simple, but solving it is not. And understanding what it means physically is even more difficult.

Few if any of us can visualize four-dimensional space, much less a curved four-dimensional space with time as one of the coordinates. None of this is surprising. It took even a great genius like Einstein ten years to develop the ideas. Possibly the simplest and best way of summarizing how gravity works in general relativity came from the physicist John Archibald Wheeler: "Matter tells space-time how to curve, and curved space tells matter how to move."

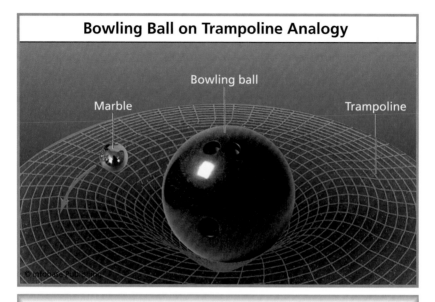

Bowling Ball on Trampoline Analogy

Marble

Bowling ball

Trampoline

© Infobase Publishing

Figure 5.7 This two-dimensional representation is analagous to the rotation of Earth around the Sun in warped space-time.

A two-dimensional analogy can help one to visualize how matter warps four-dimensional space-time. Consider a bowling ball resting in the middle of a trampoline (Figure 5.7). A marble that is rolled onto the trampoline will follow a curved path around the massive bowling ball. No force other than gravity is acting on the marble, it is simply following the path of least resistance. The marble's trajectory depends on the degree to which space-time is warped as well as the speed of the marble. Slow marbles are deflected into a curved path around the bowling ball. Faster moving ones go into orbit.

While useful, the bowling ball–trampoline analogy can be misleading. A force is required to start the marble moving on a trampoline, but in a gravitational field in space-time, no force is required. The marble simply follows the path of least resistance.

CONCLUSION

Much of relativity theory seems farfetched. Measured times and distances vary from one reference frame to another. Objects move when no direct force is applied. So far, though, not a single experimental result has been offered to substantiate this bold theory. All of us have had a lifetime of experience with unchanging time and distance. And all of us have learned that gravity is a force that attracts bodies to one another; it is the same force that astronauts overcome on their way to orbit; it is the force that holds us to the Sun. One could hardly live on Earth without having at least an intuitive grasp of Newtonian gravity.

This chapter showed that the predictions of relativity theory and Newtonian gravitation are almost always the same. Yet the next chapter will show that when the two theories do predict different outcomes, Einstein's farfetched theory wins.

6

Relativity:
Making the Case

If you shout at your friend in the next room, he will hear you. Yet, if you shine a flashlight in his direction he will not see it. While sound waves can go around corners (and be heard by people behind a wall), light waves cannot. This fact, among others, led Isaac Newton to conclude that light was not a wave but consisted of a stream of particles he called "corpuscles."

Corpuscles, Newton believed, were small bits of matter. And because they were matter, gravity should affect them. This led Newton to an important speculation: "Do not Bodies act upon Light at a distance, and by their action bend its Rays, and is not this action . . . strongest at the least distance?"

Newton's ideas about the corpuscular nature of light were discredited almost a century later. Thomas Young's famous double-slit experiment convincingly showed that light was a wave. After another 100 years, though, the corpuscular theory made a comeback. Albert Einstein's explanation of the photoelectric effect relied on light having a particle nature. This finding resurrected the possibility that gravity could bend light.

Einstein's general theory of relativity also predicted that gravity would bend light. However, he calculated that starlight passing near the Sun would be bent twice as much as predicted by Newton's laws. Einstein encouraged astronomers to measure the

Sun's deflection of starlight. He hoped the result would confirm the general theory.

Obtaining those measurements proved difficult. The Sun is so bright that other stars cannot be seen except during a solar eclipse. Furthermore, during this time, Europe was embroiled in World War I and measuring the bending of starlight was not a high priority for most people. Einstein would have to wait. Fortunately, he was aware of another problem that Newtonian physics could not account for: a tiny discrepancy in the orbit of Mercury.

THE PROBLEM WITH MERCURY

In a simple system in which one planet orbits a much larger Sun, the laws of Kepler and Newton state that the planet should trace out an

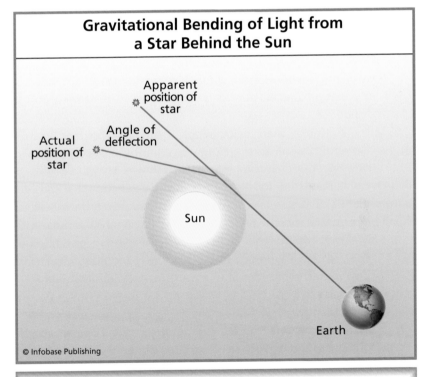

Figure 6.1   This illustration shows the gravitational bending of light from a star behind the Sun.

elliptical path around the Sun, with the Sun occupying one focus of the ellipse. The point of the planet's closest approach to the Sun is a fixed point called the **perihelion**.

Of course, real planets do not follow this script exactly. Their perihelions are not fixed. They move, or precess, around the Sun (Figure 6.2). This deviation from a simple one-planet system is mainly due to the presence of other planets whose gravitational fields perturb each other's orbits. Using Newton's laws, one can account for the precession of the perihelions of all of the planets—except Mercury.

Newton, Gravity, and Light

The German physicist Johann Georg von Soldner investigated Newton's idea about how gravity could bend light and published his findings in 1804. (Henry Cavendish, the man who provided the experimental data needed to determine Newton's gravitational constant, made a similar calculation earlier but, characteristically, he never published it.)

To make their calculations, both von Soldner and Cavendish assumed that light was composed of corpuscles of a tiny, but unknown, mass. Einstein was unaware of this work. But when he began his own calculations, he knew that light corpuscles (or photons, as they would be named later) were massless. He also knew that energy and mass were interconvertible (able to be mutually converted), as illustrated in his famous equation $E=mc^2$, and he suspected that under some conditions, pure energy might behave like mass.

Objects under the influence of gravity accelerate at the same rate, regardless of their mass. Galileo had demonstrated this when he dropped a cannonball and a musket ball from a tower and observed how they hit the ground at the same time. Therefore, Einstein did not need to know the effective mass of a photon. Employing classical

Even after taking into account the effect of gravity from all known sources, Mercury obstinately refused to obey Newton's laws. The difference between its perihelion's observed precession and the calculated one was small, only 43 arc-seconds per century. But the measurements were so accurate, even in the nineteenth century, that astronomers knew their observations were at odds with the Newtonian prediction.

The problem interested Jean Joseph Le Verrier, the French astronomer who had tackled the problem of the erratic orbit of Uranus. Le Verrier had predicted that an undiscovered planet was the

Newtonian physics, he came up with an approximate formula for calculating the deflection of starlight by the Sun:

$$A = 2Gm_2/dc^2$$

Here, A is the angle of deflection of starlight by the Sun, G is the gravitational constant, m_2 is the mass of the Sun, d is the closest distance between the incoming starlight and the Sun's center of gravity, and c is the speed of light in a vacuum.

Plugging in the numbers, Einstein found that in a Newtonian world, the Sun should deflect the starlight grazing its surface by 0.9 **arc-seconds**. (Although he did not know it, this was the same number that von Soldner had come up with over one hundred years earlier.) The calculated deflection is tiny. One second of arc is only 1/3,600 of a degree. Nevertheless, it was measurable with the telescopes available at the time.

Keep in mind that the calculation for the Newtonian bending of light is problematic at best. We do not live in a Newtonian universe. And just how much gravity might bend light in that universe (if at all) is unknown.

Still, Einstein's calculation is what astronomers in the early twentieth century used as the Newtonian prediction for the deflection of light. And that was the angle that the prediction of general relativity would be compared to.

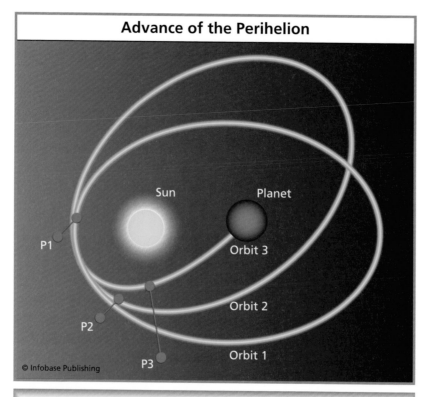

Advance of the Perihelion

Sun

Planet

P1

Orbit 3

Orbit 2

P2

P3

Orbit 1

© Infobase Publishing

Figure 6.2 As a planet orbits the Sun, it does not perfectly retrace the same orbit each time. Instead, it swings around over time. Thus, the perihelion—the point on its orbit when the planet is closest to the Sun—advances. The amount of advance shown here is greatly exaggerated.

cause of Uranus' erratic orbit. Shortly afterward, that new planet—Neptune—was spotted by astronomers.

Fresh from that success, Le Verrier turned to the dilemma posed by the orbit of Mercury. He applied the same logic that worked so well in explaining the deviant orbit of Uranus. The orbit of Mercury, he announced in 1860, was being perturbed by the presence of a never-seen planet, which he named Vulcan.

Several astronomers reported sighting the planet, but none of the sightings were ever confirmed. Le Verrier died believing that Vulcan existed, and the idea was not completely discarded until

1915, when Albert Einstein applied the general theory of relativity to the orbit of Mercury.

After years of grueling work, after numerous false starts and disappointments, Einstein was ready to test his general theory of relativity and find out if it could account for an astronomical fact that Newton's laws could not. On November 18, 1915, he used his equations to calculate the precession of Mercury's perihelion. The answer came out 43 arc-seconds per century, the same result that astronomers had arrived at after decades of observation.

Einstein was elated. "I was beside myself with joyous excitement," he said. His colleague and biographer Abraham Pais knew Einstein's feelings about the matter. "This discovery was, I believe, by far the strongest emotional experience in Einstein's scientific life, perhaps in all his life," Pais wrote in his 2000 book *The Genius of Science: A Portrait Gallery*.

Einstein was aware that his general theory was much more than an ordinary scientific breakthrough. He had rewritten the most fundamental laws of physics. Other scientists were also aware of the magnitude of Einstein's accomplishment. P.A.M. Dirac, a brilliant and mathematically talented theoretical physicist, called relativity theory "probably the greatest scientific discovery ever made." None of this made Einstein the household name he would soon become. That would take another experiment.

BENDING LIGHT

Einstein knew that the next test of general relativity would be the bending of starlight by the Sun. His theory predicted twice as much deflection as Newton's gravitational theory. Like the precession of Mercury, the difference between the predictions was small but measurable. To make the measurements, though, four conditions had to be met: a multitude of background stars must be located behind the Sun to ensure that rays of light from several stars would graze its surface; a clear sky was required to photograph the stars' apparent positions; of course, there also had to be a solar eclipse; and, finally, World War I had to end to allow the travel that would be necessary to perform the experiment.

The Other Vulcan

Orbiting a star about 16 light-years from Earth, is another planet Vulcan, one that is better known than the one proposed by Le Verrier. It is the planet popularized in the *Star Trek* series of television shows, movies, and books.

Vulcan is the home of Mr. Spock, the pointy-eared alien who routinely saves the crew of the space ship *Enterprise* from disaster. Spock's planet is a bit hotter than Earth, but it is inhabitable with a landscape that resembles Earth. Le Verrier's Vulcan, however, lies inside the orbit of Mercury. And it would be unbearably hot and totally lifeless. In fact, the two Vulcans have only one thing in common: Both are fictional.

Figure 6.3 Mr. Spock, portrayed by Leonard Nimoy, gives the Vulcan salute.

It was almost four years after Einstein's "joyous excitement" over his correct prediction of Mercury's orbit before astronomers had a decent chance to make the measurements Einstein wanted. The occasion was the solar eclipse expected on May 29, 1919.

This eclipse offered an exceptional opportunity to make the measurements because the Sun would be in front of an unusually bright group of stars. During the eclipse, many stars would be visible, and their positions could be measured and compared to control photos showing their positions when their rays were not affected by the Sun's gravitational field.

Plans to observe the eclipse were formalized after the armistice of 1918 ended the war. Two expeditions were mounted. One of them was led by the English astronomer Arthur Stanley Eddington who had been impressed by Einstein's work and was the person most interested in testing the new theory. Eddington led one expedition to Principe, an island off west coast of Africa; the other one headed for Brazil. Both teams had difficulties with their delicate telescopes and cameras. When the big day arrived, Principe was cloudy and rainy and Eddington managed to get only two usable photographs. The other team's main telescope worked poorly in the Amazonian heat and produced blurry photos. Only a smaller backup scope gave usable results.

After he returned to England, Eddington checked and double-checked the results. His team came up with a deflection of 1.61 arc-seconds. The Brazil expedition measured 1.98 arc-seconds. Einstein's predicted value of 1.74 arc-seconds was well within the 95% confidence range of both sets of measurements, while the Newtonian prediction of 0.87 arc-seconds was not. The general theory of relativity—first tested on the orbit of Mercury—was again verified.

Einstein took the news calmly. "I knew the theory was correct," he told a graduate student on the day the results arrived in Germany. He might have been (or pretended to be) nonchalant, but the rest of the war-weary world was looking for something to celebrate. Headlines everywhere carried the news. "New Theory of the Universe, Newtonian Ideas Overthrown" blared *The Times* of London. The *New York Times* followed with "Einstein Theory Triumphs." Einstein became a celebrity of the first order, as recognizable as any movie star.

Einstein deserved his fame. His theory did not just explain new data. It gave scientists a whole new way of looking at the world. So far, his new theory had accounted for only a few minor discrepancies in Newtonian physics. But the general theory would later be used to probe the deepest secrets of the universe.

However, applying the general theory to ordinary problems of physics was difficult and time consuming. Furthermore, Newton's laws work just fine in most circumstances. The next chapter will show how an apparent anomaly in the law of gravity led astronomers to one of the most surprising discoveries in all of science. Most of the universe, they now believe, is invisible.

7

Dark Matter, Dark Energy

Albert Einstein's theory of relativity superseded Isaac Newton's law of gravitational attraction. Nevertheless, Newton's equation, which relates the force of attraction between two bodies to their masses divided by the square of the distance between them, is simple, easy to use, and accurate enough for most applications. For that reason, scientists use it for almost all routine work, such as determining the speed a rocket must reach to put a satellite in orbit or predicting the motions of stars and planets.

In fact, in all but the most extreme cases of high gravity where the theory of relativity is required, Newton's law has stood the test of time for over 300 years. Still, like all scientific theories, new data should, and will, encourage scientists to challenge it. The first serious questions about Newton's law did not surface until the twentieth century. They started with a man who was studying galaxy clusters, some of the largest structures in the universe.

ONE CRANKY ASTRONOMER

Few people outside of astronomy have heard of Fritz Zwicky. By all accounts, he was brilliant, irascible, opinionated, eccentric, and full of ideas, both good and goofy. He loved to disparage the views of his

Figure 7.1 Among Swiss astronomer Fritz Zwicky's creative ideas was the possibility of rearranging the planets within our solar system. In the 1960s, he discussed how the whole solar system could possibly be moved like a giant spaceship to travel to other stars. He suggested that this might be achieved by firing pellets into the Sun to produce fusion explosions.

colleagues, whom he referred to as "spherical" jerks. (The word *jerks* was not the noun used by Zwicky, whose language was a bit saltier, but it gets the idea across.) Why spherical? Because, he loved to say, they were jerks no matter which way you looked at them.

Zwicky was born in Bulgaria in 1898 and received a first-class education in mathematics and physics. He came to the California Institute of Technology in 1925 to work in theoretical quantum mechanics. Still, being Zwicky, he did not stick to the subject matter. Instead, he became interested in astrophysics and devoted much of his research to that branch of astronomy.

In the early 1930s, Zwicky was studying the motions of the galaxies in the Coma cluster. He observed that the galaxies were moving faster than expected. At those speeds, there was not enough mass in the galaxy cluster to provide the gravitational force needed to keep the outermost galaxies from flying off into empty space. What, Zwicky wondered, was holding the cluster together?

In his hypothesis, which he published in a Swiss journal, Zwicky proposed that the force holding the Coma cluster together was ordinary gravity, much of which arose from unseen matter, which he called *dunkle Materie*—**dark matter**. This startling conjecture was greeted with deafening silence by his colleagues. Perhaps because of his high-handed ways or because many of his other notions were outlandish, Zwicky's idea about the existence of dark matter was largely ignored.

ENTER VERA RUBIN

Scientists do not come from a single mold. Galileo, for example, was a gregarious man about town, while Newton was quiet, reclusive, and vindictive. Einstein was an outgoing Bohemian, readily available to reporters. The person who painstakingly collected the data needed to turn Zwicky's speculations about dark matter into a scientifically sound hypothesis was his opposite in manner—mild, modest, and unassuming. Her name is Vera Cooper Rubin, and her work led to one of the important astronomical discoveries of the twentieth century.

Even as a child Rubin was enchanted by the stars. She majored in astronomy at Vassar and graduated in three years. In 1948, she

Figure 7.2 By studying rotation curves, American astronomer Vera Cooper Rubin discovered the discrepancy between the predicted angular motion of the galaxies and the observed motion.

applied to Princeton, a center of astrophysics and her first choice for graduate school, but Princeton turned her down. In those days, Princeton did not admit women into their astrophysics program and would not until 1971.

Undeterred, Cooper, who got married and changed her name to Vera Rubin, pursued her dream and got her Ph.D. from Georgetown University, working for the unconventional, fun-loving Russian scientist George Gamow. For the next ten years, she held various academic positions at Georgetown. Finally, she found her permanent home at the Department of Terrestrial Magnetism at the Carnegie Institution of Washington (now known as the Carnegie Institute for Science).

After settling in at Carnegie, Rubin turned her attention to measuring the **rotation curve** of Andromeda, the spiral galaxy nearest us. She knew what to expect. Astronomers could calculate a rotation curve for a spiral galaxy based on principles laid down centuries earlier by Kepler and Newton.

Spiral galaxies are shaped like flattened disks. The bright center section where most of the stars are concentrated is called the bulge. In most cases, two curving arms radiate out from the bulge, creating an image that resembles water swirling down a drain.

Our Nearest Neighbor

Andromeda is a typical spiral galaxy, similar to our own Milky Way—except it is bigger. In fact, everything about Andromeda is overwhelming. It is the nearest galaxy to Earth but it is still 2.5 million light years away. That's quite a distance, about 1.47×10^{19} miles (2.37×10^{19} km), which in ordinary numbers is 14,700,000,000,000,000,000 miles. The Andromeda galaxy is about 200,000 light years in diameter and is estimated to contain 1 trillion stars.

In addition to its stars, observers have discovered a massive black hole near the center of Andromeda. Its mass is a whopping 140 million times greater than the mass of our Sun. Everything about Andromeda is big.

Figure 7.3 Chandra observations of the massive spiral galaxy NGC 5746 revealed a large halo of hot gas (blue) surrounding the optical disk of the galaxy (white). The halo extends more than 60,000 light years on either side of the disk of the galaxy.

Most of the mass of a spiral galaxy is concentrated in the bulge. The stars and gas clouds in the galaxy rotate around the center of the bulge, just as the planets of the solar system revolve around the Sun. The rotational speed of the galaxy can be calculated at increasing distances from the center and plotted on a graph. The end product is called a galaxy rotation curve (Figure 7.4).

The initial sharp rise of speeds in the rotation curve is due to the motion of matter inside the bulge itself. If one assumes that the

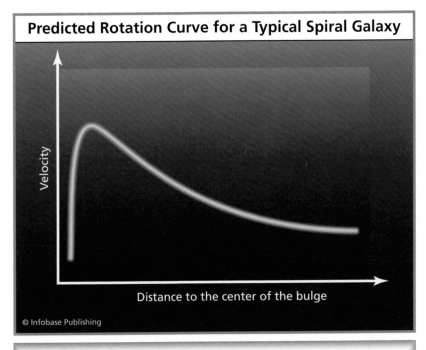

Predicted Rotation Curve for a Typical Spiral Galaxy

Velocity

Distance to the center of the bulge

© Infobase Publishing

Figure 7.4   The rotational speed of the galaxy can be calculated at increasing distances from the center and plotted on a graph.

stars and gases within the bulge are evenly distributed, then the gravitational pull on a given star can be thought of as acting from a single point in the bulge with a mass equal to the sum of the masses of all the matter inside the star's orbit.

Now, assume the galactic bulge is a sphere. The volume (Vol) of a sphere increases as the cube of the radius (r) as given below.

$$Vol = 4\pi r^3/3$$

Assuming the density inside the bulge is uniform, then the bulge's mass must increase at the same rate the volume does. Thus, the attractive mass pulling on a star orbiting in the bulge will increase with the cube of the distance of that star from the center. For a body in a circular orbit, the equation relating its speed to the mass of the object about which it is orbiting is the following:

$$v = (GM/r)^{1/2}$$

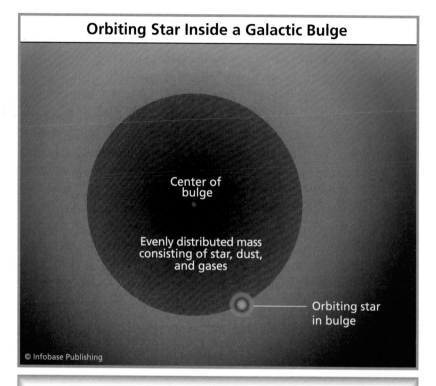

Orbiting Star Inside a Galactic Bulge

Center of
bulge

Evenly distributed mass
consisting of star, dust,
and gases

Orbiting star
in bulge

© Infobase Publishing

Figure 7.5 The force of gravity acting on an orbiting star within a galactic bulge arises from the sum of all of the masses of the stars and other matter inside the orbit of the star. The system acts as though its mass was concentrated in a single point near the center of the bulge.

where v is the speed, G is the gravitational constant, M is the mass of the bulge inside the star's orbit, and r is the radius of the orbit. Mass M in this equation increases as r^3, which is faster than r. So, the orbital speed of a star inside the bulge will increase as its distance from the center increases. This is reflected in the initial sharp rise of the graph in Figure 7.4.

Outside the bulge, the mass-distance relationship produces the opposite effect. Because the density of matter outside the bulge is much lower, increasing distance from the bulge adds little new mass. Thus, mass M in the equation can be treated as a constant. This means that the gravitational attraction between the bulge and the outlying stars falls off as the square root of the distance between them increases, as shown in the following equation:

$$v \propto 1/r^{1/2}$$

This decrease in speed as distance from the attracting body increases is exactly what one finds in our own solar system. For example, Mercury, the planet closest to the Sun, zips around it at 107,000 miles per hour (172,200 km/hr), while distant Pluto moves at a leisurely 10,500 miles per hour (16,900 km/hr).

Vera Rubin was familiar with the theory of spiral galaxy rotation. Therefore, she knew what to expect when she began measuring the speeds of the hot gases on the outskirts of the Andromeda galaxy. But the speeds she measured did not fit the theory. Instead of falling off, the speeds of the outer stars and gases remained almost constant, no matter how far they were from the galaxy's bulge. The measured rotation curve for a typical spiral galaxy can be compared to the calculated rotation curve given earlier (Figure 7.6).

What was going on? Like any good scientist, Rubin immediately suspected that Andromeda was an oddball, some kind of outlier. If so, then speed measurements of the rotations of other spiral galaxies should give the curves predicted by theory. She and her colleagues embarked on an ambitious project to measure the rotation speeds of other spiral galaxies. The results were the same. The stars and gases at the edge of the galaxies were rotating faster than expected. At those speeds, Newton's law predicts that the outermost stars should be shooting off into space. Yet something was holding them in the galaxy.

Fritz Zwicky's work with a galaxy cluster had led him to speculate that the glue holding it together was gravitational force. This force was due to the presence of an unseen substance that he called dark matter. Could that same mysterious stuff be playing a similar role in spiral galaxies?

WHAT IS DARK MATTER?

By the beginning of the twenty-first century, most astronomers and cosmologists believed that the answer to the question posed by Zwicky and Rubin was yes—the universe contained a substance called dark matter. In fact, according to a recent estimate by the National Aeronautics and Space Administration (NASA), 23% of the universe is dark matter. Much of the rest is a mysterious form

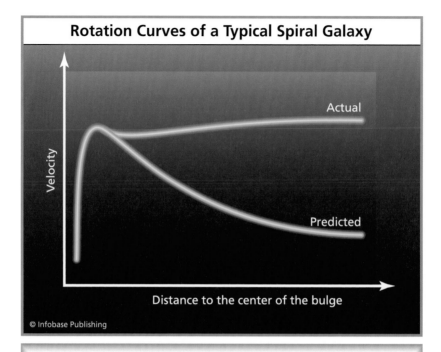

Rotation Curves of a Typical Spiral Galaxy

Actual

Velocity

Predicted

Distance to the center of the bulge

© Infobase Publishing

Figure 7.6 This graph shows the predicted and actual (observed) rotation curves of a typical spiral galaxy. The discrepancy between the curves is attributed to dark matter.

of energy that permeates space called **dark energy**. The ordinary matter—the stuff that you, Earth, and the stars are made from—that scientists once thought was the entire universe has now been relegated to a bit part, amounting to only about 5% of all matter and energy.

Although most scientists agree that dark matter exists, there is little agreement about what it is. One possibility is that dark matter could be cold ordinary matter. Cool objects do not glow and would thus be invisible in a faraway galaxy such as Andromeda. Planets, for instance, could be the dark matter or other low-luminosity objects such as **dwarf stars**, **neutron stars**, or black holes.

WIMPs (Weakly Interacting Massive Particles) are another possibility. They are a class of particles that have never been directly detected because they interact only weakly with other forces and not

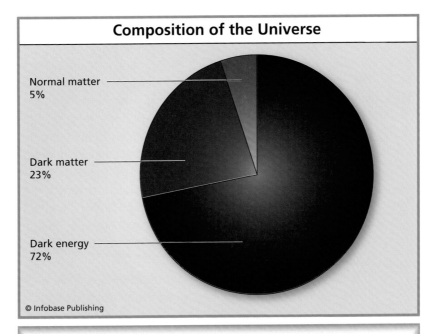

Composition of the Universe

Normal matter
5%

Dark matter
23%

Dark energy
72%

© Infobase Publishing

Figure 7.7 The universe is made up of 72% dark energy, which is a hypothetical form of energy that increases the rate of expansion of the universe.

at all with electromagnetic radiation. Consequently, they cannot be seen or detected by normal means.

Standard particle physics cannot account for the existence of a particle with all the properties of WIMPs. Despite that, many scientists believe they are good candidates for dark matter. But until someone can detect them, doubts about their existence will remain. As one might expect, many experiments are underway to find WIMPs.

A final candidate for dark matter is in many ways the most interesting. Its story starts with the acerbic genius Wolfgang Pauli. Pauli is most famous for his exclusion principle, a cornerstone of quantum theory. But he is also famous for his put-downs. "So young and already so unknown," he once said of an aspiring physicist. During a visit the United States, he lamented, "It is easy to earn much money in America but difficult to spend it in pleasant ways."

A Dark, Lonely Universe

The universe used to look like a simpler, more comfortable place. It started with the Big Bang. From this infinitely small beginning, the universe expanded. For a long time, scientists believed that, under the influence of gravity, the expansion would slow and the universe would eventually begin to contract. It would grow smaller and smaller, and finally end up as the infinitely dense point from which it came. This process, from Big Bang to Big Crunch, was a nice story with a beginning, a middle, and an end. However, recent discoveries indicate that the universe may not be following that neat script.

Astronomers began to question the Big Crunch finale in 1998. While observing a class of violently exploding stars called **supernovae**, they discovered that the universe was not only expanding (as they expected) but expanding at an increasing rate (which they definitely did not expect). This was a disturbing development. What was powering the accelerating rate of expansion? It took no great leap to name the cause. Dark energy fit the bill perfectly. But figuring out exactly what dark energy is continues to stymie scientists.

One can infer the existence of dark matter from its gravitational effects on ordinary matter. Yet dark energy has no such effect. Astronomers believe that it is distributed uniformly through space, although beyond that, its physical nature remains a mystery.

The discovery of dark energy has caused many cosmologists to radically alter their views about the future of the universe. We no longer have to worry about the Big Crunch, they say, but as time passes, everything will move away from everything else at a faster and faster rate. The friendly stars in our night sky will fade, along with ours, and finally disappear, leaving us in a dark, lonely cosmos.

In addition to being a sharp wit, Pauli was also an outstanding theoretician. In 1930, to balance the energy gained and lost in certain types of radioactive decay, he predicted the existence of a new, never-detected subatomic particle. His analysis indicated that this hypothetical particle would have no electrical charge. The physicist Enrico Fermi gave it the name **neutrino**, which is Italian for "little neutral one."

Twenty-six years after Pauli's prediction, scientists finally found a few of the ghostly particles. They were discovered by Clyde Cowan and Frederick Reines who were working at the Atomic Energy Commission's site near Aiken, South Carolina. Theory predicted that the site's nuclear reactor would produce trillions of neutrinos every second. Using a huge detector placed near the reactor, the two scientists managed to corral enough neutrinos to confirm Pauli's prediction.

Although elusive, neutrinos are not rare. Physicists have calculated that there are billions of times more neutrinos in the universe than ordinary particles. In fact, if you hold out your hand, billions of them will pass though it in a second or two. They also pass through your body, Earth, and everything else, rarely interacting with anything.

Early on, neutrinos were thought to be massless and travel at the speed of light. Recently, though, some physicists have begun to question that supposition. Neutrinos are so numerous that if they had even a tiny **at-rest mass**, those minuscule particles could add up to be the dark matter that holds huge galaxies and galactic clusters together. Because they are so small, capturing a neutrino and weighing it directly is out of the question. So, scientists have tried to measure their speeds. If the neutrino has a nonzero mass, then Einstein's relativity requires it to travel at a speed less than the speed of light. The results so far have not produced a definitive value for the speed of a neutrino. Until more precise experiments come along, neutrinos will remain a good, but unproved candidate, for dark matter.

WAS NEWTON WRONG?

The presence of dark matter—be it the cold, ordinary stuff, WIMPs, or neutrinos—can explain why stars and galaxies rotate as they do. But a few physicists think that attributing gravitational deviations to undetected matter is inelegant. What, they wonder, if it turns out that Newton's (and Einstein's) laws are not the whole story? In 1983,

Mordehai Milgrom, a physicist at the Weizmann Institute in Israel, developed a modified version of Newton's law of gravity, known as **MOND (MOdified Newtonian Dynamics)**. MOND solved the rotation problem of spiral galaxies without the need for dark matter.

According to Milgrom, Newton's laws, so reliable here on Earth, begin to break down at the huge distances encountered in galaxies and galactic clusters. Milgrom suggested that under those conditions, gravity is so weak that it no longer obeys Newton's second law of motion, which relates force to mass and acceleration. Instead of being directly proportional to acceleration, as specified by Newton, MOND holds that force is proportional to the square of acceleration. This means that the force required to produce a given acceleration is always less than the force required by Newton's law. By applying Milgrom's theory, it can be shown that all of the outlying stars in a spiral galaxy should have the same rotational velocity, which is, of course, what Vera Rubin found.

The idea that Newton's laws might be wrong is big news but not so improbable that one can dismiss it out of hand. After all, Einstein showed that those laws are incomplete, special cases of the more general laws of relativity. Nonetheless, few physicists have embraced Milgrom's theory.

The main reason for their doubts was expressed by the cosmologist Anthony Aguirre. "MOND," he writes, "....explains only what it was expressly designed to explain." In other words, MOND neatly predicts the velocity of stars and gases in the outer reaches of a spiral galaxy because that is what Milgrom formulated it to do. MOND has no theoretical underpinning. It was devised to fit the existing data.

This empirical approach is not unusual in science. Kepler came up with his laws of planetary motion this way. The question is, does MOND make other predictions and are those predictions accurate? As of now, the data are inconclusive, enabling its proponents to say yes and its opponents to say no. Clearly, more time is required for a definitive answer. So far, though, most scientists believe that dark matter explains the motion of galaxies and galaxy clusters better than MOND.

The next chapter will move away from the mysteries of dark matter to investigate even more surprising artifacts of gravity. Scientists, following up on an idea of Einstein's, have learned to use the collective gravity of billions of stars as a telescope to probe the secrets of the universe. They have also discovered the existence of bizarre, super-dense stars and even denser black holes. These black holes are the darkest objects in the universe, the products of gravity so intense that nothing can escape its grasp.

8

Extreme Gravity

In 1912, three years before he finished working out the final equations of general relativity, Einstein showed how a star could act as a magnifying lens. This was not an unreasonableidea because ordinary optical lenses bend light, just as gravity does. Therefore, Einstein reasoned, it should be possible to use gravity as a lens.

EINSTEIN'S TELESCOPE

Of course, the physics behind the two types of lenses is entirely different. Optical lenses depend on refraction, meaning the change in direction of an electromagnetic wave when it passes from one substance to another—from air to glass, for example. Gravitational lensing occurs when two massive bodies (or groups of bodies), such as stars, galaxies, or galaxy clusters, line up relative to Earth. Light from the more distant source curves around the matter between it and Earth. The light is actually following a straight line. The curve is due to the warping of space-time by the massive object(s) between Earth and the distant stars (Figure 8.1).

Unlike optical lenses, which can be machined and assembled to order, gravitational lenses require scientists to use whatever nature lines up. Although astronomers speculated for years about the possibility of gravitational lenses, they were unable to locate one. Finally, though, they did find one thanks to the discovery of an astronomical curiosity called the **quasar** or quasi-stellar object.

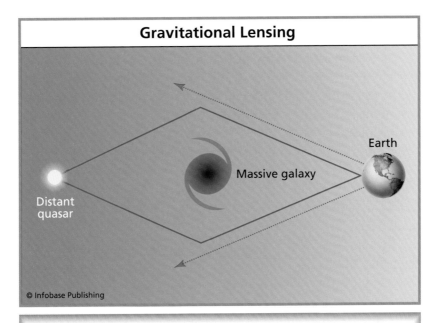

Gravitational Lensing

Earth

Massive galaxy

Distant
quasar

© Infobase Publishing

Figure 8.1 In this example of gravitation lensing, a massive galaxy
lies between Earth and a quasar, a bright, distant celestial body. The
dashed lines show two directions the light can take to reach Earth. The
result can be two distinct images.

Quasars are the most energetic bodies in the universe. They are
associated with the super massive black holes that lie in the center of
many galaxies. Billions of years ago, when the universe was younger,
these black holes were eating everything around them. The matter
falling into them emitted enormous amounts of high-energy electromagnetic radiation, which is the identifying signature of a quasar.
The more luminous ones are brighter than a trillion Suns. Astronomers today can see quasars that lie halfway across the universe.

In 1979, astronomers sighted a double quasar, a rarity. Both quasars were located about 9 billion light years from Earth. They had
to be quasars because no stars would be visible from that far away.
An analysis of the two quasars' spectra showed them to be identical.
However, this was impossible: Two quasars with exactly the same
spectra are about as likely as two humans with exactly the same fin-
gerprints. Soon, astronomers realized that they were looking at two

images of the same object. The sighting was the product of a gravitational lens.

Gravitational lenses can do strange things. The images produced depend on the exact alignment and distances of the bodies. For instance, in Figure 8.1, the observer sees two images of the same body. Yet an observer might see four images as light curves around the lensing body.

A spectacular example of quadruple imaging is the Einstein Cross (Figure 8.2). The Cross is actually four images of one quasar located about 8 billion light years from Earth. The object in the center of the photograph is the lens, a galaxy about 400 million light years away.

The Einstein Cross is a relatively simple example of gravitational lensing, but most of these images are not that easy to interpret. One complicating factor is dark matter. Because these lenses are artifacts of gravity, the presence of dark matter affects how they work. The combination of ordinary and dark matter can produce bewildering and distorted images. Yet under the proper conditions of location, distance, and alignment, gravitational lenses can do exactly what optical lenses do—concentrate light to produce clear, magnified images of distant objects. Using gravity in this creative way enables astronomers to peer deeper into the universe and has earned these lenses their own name: "Einstein's telescopes."

A STAR IS BORN

Nowhere is gravity more important than in the stars. It prevents the planets, including our own, from flying off into deep space. Equally important, gravity forms the stars. It also holds them together and plays a starring role in their afterlife.

Space is not a perfect vacuum. It is filled with an extremely dilute mixture of gases and dust called the **interstellar medium**. One cubic centimeter of space contains, on average, about one atom. (In contrast, one cubic centimeter of the air we breathe contains about 25,000,000,000,000,000,000 molecules.) Fortunately, the distribution of molecules is uneven or else the universe would be a huge bowl of thin soup. It is these inhomogeneities, coupled with the attractive action of gravity, that leads some molecules to clump together. This lumpiness can give birth to a star.

Gravitational Lens G2237+0305

Figure 8.2 The four points in this image of Einstein's Cross are images of a single, distant quasar.

About 1% of the interstellar medium is dust, which is made up of tiny particles of iron, carbon, and silicon compounds. The rest is primarily gaseous hydrogen (about 90%) and helium (about 10%) atoms and molecules. Over time, clouds of gas and dust condense as gravity works its magic on the tiny inhomogeneities in the distribution of interstellar matter.

As a cloud contracts, it heats up as the gravitational energy of the gases and particles is converted to kinetic energy. As the process continues, a protostar can form, which gets hotter and hotter. When the protostar's interior temperature reaches a few million degrees Celcius, nuclear fusion begins. In one common sequence of reactions, hydrogen nuclei fuse to form helium and release energy. Our own star, the Sun, is currently in this stage. Looking at that fiery ball today, it is hard to believe it all started when gravity, nature's weakest force, began pulling together a few molecules of gas and bits of dust.

Gravity's End?

Does gravity really go on forever? Newton's famous equation indicates that it does:

$$F = Gm_1m_2/d^2$$

The force between two objects decreases with the distance between them. But it never goes away. Every object in the universe attracts every other object, no matter how far apart they are. So, how is it that rockets are able to "break free" of Earth's gravity, as news anchors sometimes report, never to return?

The answer comes from the concept of **gravitational potential energy**. The change in gravitational potential energy is equal to the work required to move an object from one point to another in a gravitational field. Work is force times distance. Multiplying the equation for force from Newton's law of gravity by distance, one finds that U, the gravitational potential energy of an object of mass m_1 in the gravitational field of another object of mass m_2, is given by the following equation:

$$U = -Gm_1m_2/d$$

where G is the gravitational constant, and d is the distance between the centers of the two objects. (The minus sign indicates that the potential energy decreases—becomes more negative—as the objects approach one another.)

So, how much kinetic energy must a rocket generate to keep going forever if the only force acting on it is due to

Stars are a balance between the pull of gravity and the outward pressure exerted by the hot gases in the interior. Gravity may be a weak force, but it lasts forever. Bits of matter tug on one another forever, no matter how far apart they are. Yet the fuel for the fusion that powers the stars—the energy that holds gravity at bay—will run

Earth's gravitational field? The formula for kinetic energy is as follows:

$$E = 1/2m_1v^2$$

The minimum kinetic energy the rocket will need to overcome gravity must equal the magnitude of the gravitational potential energy at Earth's surface.

$$1/2m_1v^2 = Gm_1m_2/d$$

Factoring out the mass of the rocket ship, leaves

$$v^2 = 2Gm_2/d$$

This is the minimum speed the rocket ship must reach to overcome Earth's gravitational field. It is called the **escape velocity**. Thus,

$$v_{esc} = (2Gm_2/d)^{1/2}$$

Plugging in the numbers for Earth, one gets a speed of 25,000 miles per hour (11,200 m/sec). On the Moon, the getaway speed is less than 5,300 miles per hour (2,370 m/sec). To permanently leave the Sun, though, one must speed up to well over 1 million miles per hour. Note that the escape velocity is independent of the mass of the departing body. It is the same for a rocket ship as for a baseball. Note, too, that escape velocity is an ill-named quantity. First, it is not a velocity but a speed independent of direction. Second, one does not "escape" gravity so much as overcome it.

Now, to answer the question that started this section: Gravity does go on forever. One can never "break free" of it. But an object with enough kinetic energy can overcome it.

out. And when it does, gravity is there waiting. Under its relentless force, the star collapses.

DEATH OF A STAR

The endpoint of a star's collapse depends on its size. Stars with mass about the same as the Sun go through several stages on the way to their death, expanding and contracting and blowing off outer layers of gas as they deplete their nuclear fuel. What is finally left is the smoldering core of the gravitationally compressed star, a dense remnant of carbon and oxygen ions and electrons. The pressure that pushes back against further collapse is different from the hot gas that keeps a star shining. This pressure is due to the **Pauli exclusion principle**.

The increasing gravitational pressure in the star's remnant core squeezes the electrons together to form an electron **degenerate gas**. Because of the exclusion principle, no two electrons not clearly separated by position can occupy the same quantum state. Thus, further compression pushes the electrons into higher and higher energy levels. These high-energy, high-speed electrons strongly resist compression. This electron degeneracy pressure is present in all matter, but it is negligibly small at ordinary densities.

For stars the size of the Sun, the degeneracy pressure eventually counterbalances the force of gravity. The result is a dense Earth-sized object called a **white dwarf**. These remnant stars are a consequence of extreme gravity, which has left them with some extraordinary properties. For instance, the density of a typical white dwarf is about one million times the density of water. A teaspoon of white dwarf would weigh 5 tons.

Another curious property of degenerate matter is the relationship between size and mass. Double the mass of a normal star or an ordinary gas (or liquid or solid) at a fixed pressure and temperature and its volume will double. Double the mass of a white dwarf and its volume will decrease. This means that a larger star will form a smaller white dwarf.

The culprit behind this unusual property is gravity. More mass means higher gravity. Higher gravity produces higher density— and smaller size. In some cases, though, gravity can overcome the

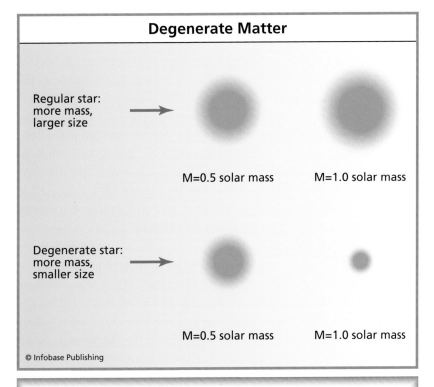

Degenerate Matter

Regular star:
more mass,
larger size

M=0.5 solar mass   M=1.0 solar mass

Degenerate star:
more mass,
smaller size

M=0.5 solar mass   M=1.0 solar mass

© Infobase Publishing

Figure 8.3   Degenerate matter is extraordinary matter created in
the cores of stars where atoms and subatomic particles are packed so
densely that the primary source of pressure is no longer thermal, but
instead quantum.

pressure of the electron degenerate gas resisting it. This occurs
when the star remnant is significantly more massive than the Sun.
This divide between ordinary white dwarfs and those that undergo
further compression is called the **Chandrasekhar limit**, named for
the Indian physicist Subrahmanyan Chandrasekhar who first proposed it.

Chandrasekhar showed that electron degeneracy pressure could
not balance the crush of gravity if the mass of a white dwarf exceeded
1.4 times the mass of the Sun. At the time, he did not speculate on
what would happen to such a star, except that it would continue to
collapse. It was only later that scientists learned the fate of star remnants with masses exceeding the Chandrasekhar limit.

THE GREATEST WONDER

On November 11, 1572, Danish astronomer Tycho Brahe left his lab, which was located in Herrevad Abbey (a monastery in present-day southern Sweden), and strolled toward the dining room for dinner. It was a clear evening, and when he glanced at the sky he saw a star he had never seen before. Tycho was the greatest astronomer of his day and was known for his careful observations. So, he knew that no star had been in that location before. It was, he wrote, "the greatest wonder that has ever showed itself in the whole of nature. . . ." It turns out that what Tycho saw was not a functioning star but one in its death throes. And scientists now know that its death was anything but gentle.

The bright object Tycho spotted was an exploding star, an event known as a supernova. These are some of the most violent happenings in the universe. Over a period of a few days or weeks, a supernova will generate enough energy to outshine an entire galaxy containing hundreds of billions of stars. This is the fate of dying stars with masses higher than the Chandrasekhar limit.

Supernovae are complex events that fall into two broad categories. (For our purposes, the several subdivisions of these categories can be ignored.) Type I supernovae typically occur when a white dwarf accumulates enough matter from another star to push it above the Chandrasekhar limit. This results in a runaway thermonuclear explosion, often leading to the complete disintegration of the star.

Type II supernovae are caused by the gravitational collapse of a star that has exhausted its fuel supply. Much of the star is blasted off into space, but a remnant is often left behind. If the mass of the remnant exceeds the Chandrasekhar limit, it collapses further. Electrons are squeezed into protons to form neutrons. The gravitational collapse may finally be halted by the pressure of the remnant's neutron degenerate gas. The result is an astounding object called a neutron star.

A neutron star has a density approaching that of an atomic nucleus. The packed-together neutrons make a white dwarf look like a ball of fluff. A typical neutron star packs an entire Sun into a sphere about 10 kilometers in diameter. This gives it an average density of about 10^{17} kilograms per cubic meter, about 100,000,000 times as dense as a white dwarf. One teaspoon of this stuff would weigh 500,000,000 tons.

This is extreme gravity. If somone dropped a baseball on a neutron star, it would reach a speed of about 1,000 miles (1,600 kilometers) per second when it hit the star's surface. This means that gravity accelerated the ball from a standstill to more than 4 million miles per hour in a three-foot drop.

There are other amazing statistics about neutron stars: for instance, their rate of rotation is very fast and their temperature is very high. However, as incredible as neutron stars are, an even more amazing entity lies beyond them. This object forms when even more massive stars collapse. When a supernova blast leaves a remnant larger than three solar masses, even the neutron degenerate gas cannot withstand the force of gravity. The star collapses further to form a black hole.

BLACK HOLES

Just a few weeks after Einstein published his general theory of relativity in 1915, Karl Schwarzschild produced the first exact solution to Einstein's equations, which showed how a star would curve space-time. At the time, World War I was under way and Schwarzschild, a distinguished physicist, was serving in the German army on the Russian front. He sent his calculations to Einstein who presented them on his behalf. To simplify the mathematics, Schwarzschild assumed that the star was perfectly spherical and not spinning. His solution details how a star (or any other spherical mass) warps space-time.

Schwarzschild's calculations revealed how the curvature of space-time becomes more pronounced near highly dense, compact objects. Most scientists at the time had no problem agreeing with that conclusion. However, when taken to the extreme, Schwarzschild's geometry made a startling prediction with which many scientists (including Einstein himself) could not agree.

The prediction indicated that any object, if sufficiently compressed, can become a black hole, a body so dense that nothing—not even light—can escape its gravity. All one has to do is shrink it below its **Schwarzchild radius**. Molecular and atomic repulsion stop Earth from shrinking to its Schwarzchild radius and becoming a black hole. Hot gases keep the Sun from that fate. Yet if you keep shrinking any object, down past its white dwarf stage, past its neutron star stage, past its Schwarzchild radius, it will turn into a black hole.

The formula for the Schwarzchild radius for any object of mass m is

$$r_s = 2Gm/c^2$$

where G is the gravitational constant and c is the speed of light in a vacuum. Upon rearranging the equation, one gets

$$c = (2Gm/r_s)^{1/2}$$

Chandrasekhar vs. Eddington

New theories are never accepted by established scientists. It's not until the old guard dies that a new theory gains prestige and recognition as the new minds, who created the theory, take their rightful positions in the institutions that only yesterday had kept them out.

It is not clear who first expressed this sentiment, but it is a deeply held belief of many young scientists. And there is no better example of the devastating effects of this truism than Arthur Stanley Eddington's treatment of Subrahmanyan Chandrasekhar.

Chandrasekhar first calculated the limit that determines the fate of white dwarf stars in 1930. The scientific community was slow to buy into his idea. To buttress his theory, the young physicist needed to show that no existing white dwarf had a mass that exceeded his limit. To make his point, Chandrasekhar determined the masses of ten white dwarfs. Every one had a mass of less than 1.4 solar masses, just as he had predicted. When he finally presented this work to the Royal Astronomical Society in 1935, he ran into the old-guard buzz saw.

This is the same relationship derived earlier in the equation for escape velocity, with the speed of light substituted for escape velocity. Its meaning is clear. When an object reaches Schwarzchild radius, the escape velocity is equal to the speed of light. And because nothing can go faster than light, nothing can escape from a body that has been compressed to its Schwarzchild radius. A black hole can be defined as any object smaller than its Schwarzchild radius.

Extremely high pressures are required to create an object that small. One would have to squeeze the Sun down from its current radius of about 434,000 to less than 2 miles (700,000 to 3 km). To make a black hole out of Earth, it would have to be compressed to the size of a pea. Still, black holes are thought to be common in the

Arthur Stanley Eddington, the preeminent astronomer in Britain at the time, attended the presentation. After Chandrasekhar's talk, he strode to the podium and attempted to demolish the young man's arguments. Eddington knew that Chandrasekhar's results implied the existence of the objects today called black holes, and he doubted that such unreasonable things could be found in a reasonable universe. He knew Chandrasekhar well and was familiar with his work. Yet, he had never expressed his reservations before this important meeting. Now, he argued strongly that Chandrasekhar's work was flawed. Then, he summarized his feelings succinctly: "I think there should be a law of Nature to prevent a star from behaving in this absurd way."

Eddington's opposition to Chandrasekhar's limit slowed the acceptance of the existence of black holes. Chandrasekhar himself was so discouraged by Eddington's ambush that he turned to other research. Over time, though, Eddington's sway diminished, and younger astrophysicists accepted the reality of black holes. Chandrasekhar was eventually rewarded with a Nobel prize for his work on the structure of stars, but he had to wait more than half a century for the honor.

universe. And scientists are getting a handle on the nature of these bizarre objects.

Black holes are black—they absorb all light that hits them. Nonrotating black holes have a spherical boundary, a surface of no return called the **event horizon**, which has a radius equal to its Schwarzchild radius. Anything that passes this horizon is forever gone. One way to understand black holes is to imagine what would happen to a person—you, for instance—as you approach the event horizon of a large black hole.

To an observer at a distance, time dilation would slow your descent toward the event horizon. However, you, falling freely through the void, would feel nothing different. Your watch would run normally, and you would not even know it when you sailed past the event horizon. Once inside, you would be pulled toward the center of the back hole. Soon, you would begin to feel a differential pull as the curve of space became significant relative to the size of your body. Then, you would be ripped to pieces.

If that seems harsh, consider what would happen if your experience was expressed in Newtonian language. If gravity sucked you into the black hole feet first, you would gradually feel your feet, which are closer to the black hole's center and subject to the strongest gravity, being pulled away from your head. Soon you would be stretched out like a rubber band. Then, you would be ripped to pieces.

Of course, all of this is speculation. Although scientists are reasonably sure about what goes on inside a black hole, no one has ever been inside one and returned to tell about it. And some features of black holes are difficult to fathom. For example, they form when matter collapses, but how far can matter collapse and where does it go? Or, to put it another way, what lies in the center of a black hole?

With nothing to stop its gravitational collapse, the mass of a black hole shrinks to an infinitely dense point. Mathematically, such a point is called a **singularity**. A simple example of a mathematical singularity is dividing by zero. What is $1/x$ when $x = 0$? No one knows; therefore, it is undefined. The same thing happens at the singularity of a black hole. Infinitely dense matter creates infinitely curved space-time. The result is the end point of extreme gravity—an undefined, chaotic, dimensionless point.

Geometry of a Black Hole

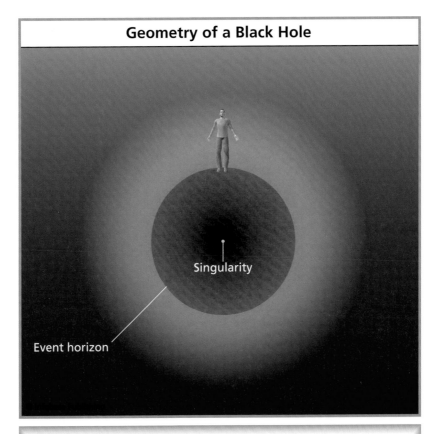

Singularity

Event horizon

Figure 8.4 This illustration of a spherical, nonrotating black hole shows the location of the singularity and the event horizon.

DO BLACK HOLES EXIST?

In 1784, English scientist John Michell (the man who designed the torsion balance) wrote a letter to Henry Cavendish (the man who weighed Earth) exploring the effect of gravity on light. Consider, Michell wrote, an object massive enough to prevent light from escaping. Nothing in Newton's laws prevented such an object from lurking somewhere in the heavens. It would not be directly visible, he hypothesized, but it might be identified by the effect of its gravitational pull on motions of other stars. Unfortunately, Michell's work was forgotten until the 1970s and played no role in the discovery of of black holes. Nevertheless, he was the first person to anticipate their existence.

Since Michell's day, many of science's top theorists have speculated about the nature of black holes. Einstein and Eddington doubted they existed. Chandrasekhar and Schwarzchild were believers. Many other distinguished scientists—among them, J. Robert Oppenheimer, who led the Manhattan Project during World War II; Stephen Hawking, who held Isaac Newton's old post of Lucasian Professor of Mathematics at Cambridge University; and John Wheeler, who coined the term *black hole*—weighed in with their ideas, calculations, and theories.

Observational astronomers, however, could add little to this debate. After all, black holes are invisible. It was not until the beginning of space-based astronomy that working astronomers began to make contributions to the debate. Telescopes that operated above Earth's atmosphere opened a new window for watching the heavens. One surprising discovery was that X-rays—which cannot penetrate Earth's atmosphere—were flashing through the universe.

Most of these X-ray emissions came from **binary stars**. Binaries are not uncommon. They are made up of two stars orbiting a common center of mass. Many of them consist of two ordinary stars and emit radiation in the visible range. But a special class of binary systems emits very high energy X-rays. The X-rays are produced by matter flowing from one star to the other. If the gravitational pull of the attracting body is strong, the gas falling in is heated to temperatures so high that it gives off X-rays. The only bodies with sufficient gravity to accelerate a gas to those speeds are very dense objects—such as white dwarfs, neutron stars, and black holes.

The first X-ray binary star was discovered in 1964 by a sounding rocket that was launched in New Mexico. The rocket's instruments detected a strong X-ray emitter, which was named Cygnus X-1, located about 6,000 light years away. Some scientists suspected that the high-energy emissions came from a black hole that was sucking in matter. The source of the emissions was the subject of a friendly wager between two prominent investigators of black holes: Stephen Hawking and Kip Thorne, a professor of theoretical physics at the California Institute of Technology.

Thorne believed that Cygnus X-1 was a black hole; Hawking disagreed. They made their bet in 1974 and, by 1990, Hawking had

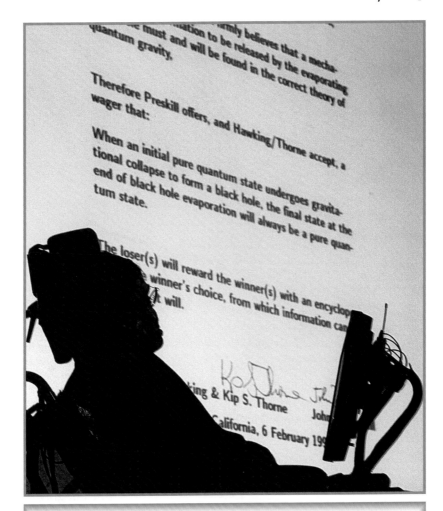

Figure 8.5   Cosmologist Stephen Hawking, shown here at a conference in July 2004, made another famous bet. This one was with American physicist John Preskill concerning the existence of a special type of singularity. The outcome is not yet decided. Here, the letter that states his bet is viewed by an audience, including Hawking himself (*in front*).

conceded: Cygnus X-1 was almost certainly a black hole. The evidence came from tracking the motion of the normal star in the binary system. Its orbit indicated that the unseen body it is locked into contained about 8.7 solar masses. That was far too massive to be a white dwarf or neutron star.

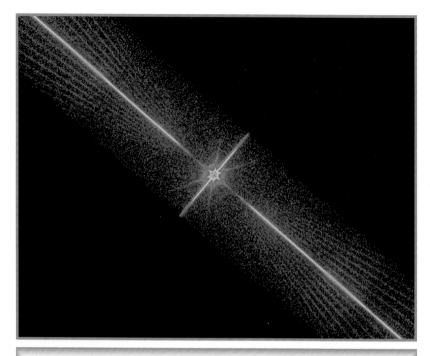

Figure 8.6 This Chandra X-ray Observatory image is a spectrum of a black hole, which is similar to the colorful spectrum of sunlight produced by a prism. The X-rays of interest are shown here recorded in the bright stripe that runs rightward and leftward from the center of the image.

Research on the X-ray emissions of binary stars was aided by the 1999 launch of the Chandra X-ray Observatory, appropriately named for Subrahmanyan Chandrasekhar. Since then, thanks to the Chandra observatory and a battery of new instruments, many other likely black holes have been identified and classified by size. The observatory has also generated spectroscopic data that allow scientists to piece together the details of how a black hole functions in a binary star.

SUMMING UP

Gravity is the weakest force in the universe, but its persistence can create spectacular effects. White dwarfs and neutron stars are formed by gravitational forces that create preposterously dense forms of matter. In the most extreme case, the gravitational force (or the curvature of space-time) is so great that it results in a black hole from which not even light can escape.

Our own earthly encounters with gravity are more mundane. They usually involve little more than huffing and puffing when we walk up a few flights of stairs or marveling at the trajectory of a well-hit baseball. We live with gravity every day, and our intuitive grasp of it tells us to avoid steep stairs if an elevator is handy and enables us to catch a fly ball—at least most of the time. So, we ordinarily ignore it.

Yet, as we age, we will inevitably tire, but gravity never does. And it will eventually have its way with us. The average person over 40 shrinks every year as gravity compresses the spine and bones. Of course, we are not as long lived as a star, so we will never shrink to a black hole. Still, as we age, those lost inches remind us of the unseen presence of the weak, but inexorable, attraction between bodies called gravity.

Glossary

acceleration   The change in velocity with time

arc-second   An angular measure equal to 1/3,600 of a degree

at-rest mass   The measure of the quantity of matter in an object that is at rest relative to the observer

binary star   A pair of stars revolving around a common center of mass

black holes   An object so dense that nothing, including light, can escape its gravity

center of mass   The point at which the entire mass of an object can be considered to be concentrated; under most conditions, an object's center of mass is also its center of gravity.

Chandrasekhar limit   The limiting mass of a white dwarf; any nonrotating white dwarf with a mass exceeding the Chandrasekhar limit of 1.4 solar masses will undergo further gravitational collapse to become a neutron star or black hole.

closed system   Sometimes called an isolated system, it is a system that does not interact with its surroundings; the mass and energy in a closed system can change from one form to another but the total must remain the same.

compound   A substance composed of two or more elements joined by chemical bonds

conservation of energy   Because mass and energy are inter-convertible, this law is better stated as the conservation of mass-energy; in an isolated system, mass-energy cannot be lost or gained.

dark energy   A hypothetical form of energy that permeates space and is causing the expansion of the universe to accelerate

dark matter Matter whose presence is inferred from its gravitational effect on stars and galaxies; dark matter has not yet been directly detected.

degenerate gas A highly dense form of matter that resists further compression because of quantum mechanical effects

dwarf star A small, cool, low-luminosity star

ellipse An oval geometric shape resembling a squashed (or elongated) circle.

electromagnetic waves Massless energy waves that travel at 3.0 x 10^8 m/sec in a vacuum.

electrostatic force The force acting between two electrically charged objects; it is many orders of magnitude stronger than the force of gravity.

element A substance that cannot be split into simpler substances by chemical means

escape velocity The minimum speed that an object must reach to overcome the gravitational attraction of another object

event horizon The point of no return of a black hole; at the event horizon, escape velocity equals the speed of light.

force The agency (symbol F) that produces acceleration in a body. Newton's second law states that F = ma, where m is the mass of the body and a is the acceleration imparted to it by force F.

frame of reference An object or person's immediate surroundings; objects that are participating in the same motion; special relativity predicts that time and distance depend on the frame of reference in which they are measured.

galaxy cluster Groups of up to a few thousand galaxies, each of which may contain billions of stars

general theory of relativity Einstein's 1915 theory that describes how mass curves space-time and how that curvature is gravity

gravitational field The region of space around a body with mass

gravitational potential energy The energy that an object possesses because of its position in a gravitational field; near the surface of Earth, where the gravitational field is constant, an object's gravitational potential energy is equal to its weight times the height to which it is lifted.

inertial reference frames   Reference frames that move in a straight line at constant velocity; the laws of special relativity hold only in these frames.

interstellar medium   The thin soup of gas and dust found between the stars

inverse square law   The law that relates the magnitude of some quantity to the reciprocal of the square of the distance between two objects; Newton's law of gravity and the law electrostatic attraction or repulsion are two examples.

Kepler's three laws of planetary motion   The three fundamental laws of planetary motion proposed by Johannes Kepler and published in the early seventeenth century that describe the orbits of planets

kinetic energy   The energy of motion; the classical equation for kinetic energy of a body is $mv^2/2$, where m is the mass of the body and v is its speed.

law of universal gravitation   Newton's law relating the force of attraction between two objects to their masses and to the inverse of the square of the distance between them

length contraction   A consequence of the special theory of relativity which predicts that the length of an object in a reference frame moving relative to an observer appears contracted in the direction of motion; the length is a maximum in the frame in which the object is at rest.

light year   The distance light travels in a vacuum in one year, about 5.9×10^{12} miles (9.5×10^{15} m)

luminiferous ether   The hypothetical medium through which light was supposed to propagate; the Michelson-Morley experiment of 1887 was unable to detect its existence.

mass   A measure of the quantity of matter in a body or its inertia (i.e., its resistance to acceleration). On Earth, weight is used to indicate the mass of an object.

MOND (MOdified Newtonian Dynamics)   The theory that force is proportional to the square of acceleration in regions where the acceleration is very low rather than directly proportional to it as specified in Newton's second law; the theory was developed to explain the anomaly in the rotation curves of spiral galaxies.

motion   The change in position of a body with time within a frame of reference; absolute motion is meaningless; only relative motion can be determined.

neap tides   A tide with a smaller than usual difference between high and low tides; neap tides occur when the Sun, Earth, and Moon form a right angle.

neutrino   An electrically neutral particle with no (or exceedingly small) at-rest mass that travels at (or very near) the speed of light; neutrinos are numerous but hard to detect.

neutron star   Extremely dense matter formed by the gravitational collapse of a white dwarf with a mass exceeding the Chandrasekhar limit of 1.4 solar masses; if the mass of the white dwarf exceeds three solar masses, it will bypass the neutron-star phase and become a black hole.

parabolic orbit   The path followed by some objects that pass near the Sun (or any massive object); comets in parabolic orbits are deflected by the Sun's gravity but are one-time events, shooting off into space after they pass the Sun never to return.

Pauli exclusion principle   Principle that states that no two electrons in an atom can possess an identical set of quantum numbers

perihelion   The point in the solar orbit of a planet (or satellite or comet) where it is nearest the Sun

principle of equivalence   Einstein's breakthrough concept that gravity is indistinguishable from an accelerating reference frame.

proportionality constant   Two quantities x and y are proportional .if there exists a constant, non-zero number in which x=Cy. In this case, C is the proportionality constant.

quasar   Distant, extraordinarily energetic sources of radiation believed to be emitted by hot gases being sucked into a black hole; the name is a contraction of "quasi-stellar" objects.

rotation curve   A plot of the rotational speeds of stars and other matter as a function of distance from the center of a spiral galaxy

scalar quantity   A quantity in which direction is either not applicable (temperature, for instance) or not specified; speed is a scalar quantity; velocity is a vector.

Schwarzchild radius   The radius of the event horizon of a black hole; any object compressed to its Schwarzchild radius becomes a black hole.

semidiurnal   Occurring twice a day

singularity   A point at which a given mathematical object is not defined; every black hole is believed to contain a singularity of infinite density.

SI units   The International System of Units, abbreviated SI from the French Le Système International d'Unités; this form of the metric system is almost universally used in science.

space-time   The combination of three-dimensional space with time; all four coordinates are required to specify an event.

special theory of relativity   The laws of physics are the same in all inertial reference frames; Einstein's general theory extended this principle to all reference frames.

spring tide   A tide with a greater than usual difference between high and low tides; spring tides occur about every two weeks, when Sun and Moon are aligned with Earth.

supernova   An exploding star that is temporarily brighter than all the stars in a galaxy

teleology   A way of thinking about the natural world which assumes that the processes of nature have a goal or a purpose

tensors   Complex mathematical entities that express relationships between vectors

tidal lock   A gravitational effect that causes one side of a rotating astronomical body to always face another, as one side of the Moon always faces Earth

time dilation   The lengthening of the time interval between two events when measured in reference frames that are different from the frame in which the event occurred

vector quantity   A quantity that specifies both magnitude and direction; force and velocity are vector quantities, but time and temperature are not.

white dwarf   A compact star with a mass below the Chandrasekhar limit of 1.4 solar masses; compact stars with masses above the limit collapse further to become neutron stars or black holes.

WIMP (Weakly Interacting Massive Particle)   A hypothetical particle that is a candidate for dark matter

Bibliography

Aczel, Amir D. *God's Equation: Einstein, Relativity, and the Expanding Universe.* New York: Dell Publishing, 1999.

The Archimedes Project. "Benedetti, Giovanni Battista." Available online. URL: http://archimedes2.mpiwg-berlin.mpg.de/archimedes_templates/biography.html?-table=archimedes_authors&author=Benedetti,%20Giovanni%20Battista

Australia Telescope Outreach and Education. "The Death of Stars I: Solar-Mass Stars." Available online. URL: http://outreach.atnf.csiro.au/education/senior/astrophysics/stellarevolution_deathlow.html

Australia Telescope Outreach and Education. "The Death of Stars II: High Mass Stars." Available online. URL: http://outreach.atnf.csiro.au/education/senior/astrophysics/stellarevolution_deathhigh.html

Bartusiak, Marcia. *Through a Universe Darkly: A Cosmic Tale of Ancient Ethers, Dark Matter, and the Fate of the Universe.* New York: HarperCollins, 1993.

Bay of Fundy Tourism. "Tides in the Bay of Fundy." Available online. URL: http://www.bayoffundytourism.com/tides/

Brau, Jim. "Astronomy 122: Birth and Death of Stars." Available online. URL: http://www.physics.uoregon.edu/~jimbrau/astr122/

Coles, Peter. "Einstein, Eddington and 1919 Eclipse." Available online. URL: http://arxiv.org/abs/astro-ph/0102462

Cooke, Donald A. *The Life & Death of Stars.* New York: Crown Publishers, 1985.

Crowther, J.G. *The Cavendish Laboratory 1874-1974.* New York: Science History Publications, 1974.

Darling, David. *Gravity's Arc: The Story of Gravity, from Aristotle to Einstein and Beyond.* New York: John Wiley & Sons, 2006.

Dovada Research Reference Library. "The Planets Solar System." Available online. URL: http://www.dovada.com/orbital_data.htm

Drake, Stillman. *Galileo at Work: His Scientific Biography.* New York: Dover Publications, 1978.

Drake, Stillman. *Galileo: A Very Short Introduction.* Oxford, U. K.: Oxford University Press, 1980, reissued 1996.

Durant, Will and Ariel. *The Story of Civilization, vol. VIII: The Age of Louis XIV.* New York: Simon and Schuster, 1963.

Ferguson, Kitty. *Tycho & Kepler: The Unlikely Partnership That Forever Changed Our Understanding of the Heavens.* New York: Walker & Company, 2002.

Ferris, Timothy. *Coming of Age in the Milky Way.* New York: William Morrow, 1988.

Ferris, Timothy. *The Whole Shebang: A State-of-the Universe(s) Report.* New York: Simon & Schuster, 1997.

Galilei, Galileo. *Dialogue Concerning the Two Chief World Systems.* New York: The Modern Library, 2001.

Galilei, Galileo. *Dialogues Concerning Two New Sciences.* Philadelphia: Running Press, 2002.

Garrison, Tom. *Oceanography: An Invitation to Marine Science.* Pacific Grove, Calif.: Brooks/Cole, 2002.

Gates, Evalyn. *Einstein's Telescope: The Hunt for Dark Matter and Dark Energy in the Universe.* New York: W.W. Norton, 2009.

Georgia State University. "Escape Velocity." Available online. URL: http://hyperphysics.phy-astr.gsu.edu/hbase/vesc.html

Georgia State University. "Halley's Comet." Available online. URL: http://hyperphysics.phy-astr.gsu.edu/hbase/solar/halley.html

Georgia State University. "Neutrino Mass?" Available online. URL: http://hyperphysics.phy-astr.gsu.edu/Hbase/particles/neutrino.html

Georgia State University. "White Dwarf." Available online. URL: http://hyperphysics.phy-astr.gsu.edu/HBASE/astro/whdwar.html

Gleick, James. *Isaac Newton.* New York: Pantheon Books, 2003.

Isaacson, Walter. *Einstein: His Life and Universe.* New York: Simon and Schuster, 2007.

Johnson, George. *The Ten Most Beautiful Experiments.* New York: Alfred A. Knopf, 2008.

Jungnickel, Christa and Russell McCormmach. *Cavendish.* Philadelphia: The American Philosophical Society, 1996.

Koppel, Tom. *Ebb and Flow: Tides and Life on Our Once and Future Planet.* Toronto, Canada: The Dundurn Group, 2007.

Lally, Sean P. "Henry Cavendish and the Density of the Earth." *The Physics Teacher* 37 (January 1999): 34–37.

Lilienfeld, Scott O. and Hal Arkowitz. "Lunacy and the Full Moon: Does a Full Moon Really Trigger Strange Behavior?" *Scientific American Mind* 20 (February 2009): 64–65.

Milgrom, Mordehai. "Does Dark Matter Really Exist?" *Scientific American* 287 (August 2002): 42–52.

NASA. "What's the Universe Made Of?" Available online. URL: http://map. gsfc.nasa.gov/universe/uni_matter.html

Newton, Isaac. *The Principia: Mathematical Principles of Natural Philosophy*, translated by I. Bernard Cohen and Anne Whitman. Berkeley: University of California Press, 1999.

Nicolson, Iain. *Dark Side of the Universe: Dark Matter, Dark Energy, and the Fate of the Cosmos*. Baltimore: The Johns Hopkins University Press, 2007.

Mihos, Chris. Department of Astronomy, Case Western Reserve University: "Gravity." Available online. URL: http://burro.astr.cwru.edu/ Academics/Astr201/Motion/motion2.html

Pais, Abraham. *The Genius of Science: A Portrait Gallery*. New York: Oxford University Press, 2000.

Pew Research Center Publications. "How the Public Resolves Conflicts Between Faith and Science." Available online. URL: http://pewresearch. org/pubs/578/when-science-and-faith-compete-faith-usually-wins

Pogge, Richard. Ohio State University: "Astronomy 161: Lecture 20: Tides." Available online. URL: http://www.astronomy.ohio-state.edu/~pogge/ Ast161/Unit4/tides.html

Reddy, M.P.M. *Descriptive Physical Oceanography*. Exton, Pennsylvania: A.A. Balkema Publishers, 2001.

Scharringhausen, Britt. Cornell University: "Curious About Astronomy? Is the Moon Moving Away from the Earth?" Available online. URL: http:// curious.astro.cornell.edu/question.php?number=124

Schutz, Bernard. *Gravity from the Ground Up*. Cambridge, U.K.: Cambridge University Press, 2003.

Sheehan, William, Nicholas Kollerstrom, and Craig B. Waff. "The Case of the Pilfered Planet: Did the British Steal Neptune." *Scientific American* 291 (December 2004): 90–99.

Simanek, Donald. "Tidal Misconceptions." Available online. URL: http:// www.lhup.edu/~dsimanek/scenario/tides.htm

The Royal Society. "History of the Society." Available online. URL: http:// royalsociety.org/page.asp?id=1058

Suite 101. "A Visual Representation of Curved Spacetime." Available online. URL: http://www.suite101.com/view_image.cfm/311740

Thorne, Kip S. *Black Holes & Time Warps: Einstein's Outrageous Legacy*. New York: W. W. Norton & Company, 1994.

Tucker, James. "Strange Case of Ye Olde Tide Mill." Available online. URL: http://www.hampton.lib.nh.us/HAMPTON/history/ourtown/tidemill.htm

Tyson, Peter. "Galileo's Battle for the Heavens: His Big Mistake." Available online. URL: http://www.pbs.org/wgbh/nova/galileo/mistake.html

University of Cambridge, Department of Physics. "The History of the Cavendish." Available online. URL: http://www.phy.cam.ac.uk/history/

University of Winnipeg. "Theoretical Physics: Gravitational Potential Energy." Available online. URL: http://theory.uwinnipeg.ca/mod_tech/node57.html

White, Michael. *Isaac Newton: The Last Sorcerer*. Reading, Mass.: Perseus Books, 1997.

Wolfson, Richard. *Simply Einstein: Relativity Demystified*. New York: W.W. Norton, 2003.

Further Resources

Calaprice. Alice, ed. *Dear Professor Einstein: Albert Einstein's Letters To and from Children*. Amherst, New York: Prometheus Books, 2002.

Clement, Hal. *Mission of Gravity*. London: Gollancz, 2000 (Originally published in 1953).

Cook, Alan H. *Edmond Halley: Charting the Heavens and the Seas*. New York: Oxford University Press, 1998.

Einstein, Albert. *Relativity: The Special and General Theory*. New York: Wings Books, 1952 (Originally published in 1916).

Foland, Andrew Dean. *Energy*. New York: Chelsea House, 2007.

Goodwin, Richard N. *The Hinge of the World: A Drama*. New York: Farrar, Straus & Giroux, 1998.

Greene, Brian. "Gravity: From Newton to Einstein." Available online. URL: http://www.youtube.com/watch?v=O-p8yZYxNGc&NR=1

Hawking, Stephen W. *A Brief History of Time: From the Big Bang to Black Holes*. New York: Bantam Books, 1988.

Web Sites

A.J. Design Software: "Gravity Equations Formulas Calculator"
URL: http://www.ajdesigner.com/phpgravity/newtons_law_gravity_equation_force.php

Plug in your weight in newtons or pounds or whatever and the calculator will tell you the force of attraction between you and any other object you choose.

Chandra X-ray Observatory: "Supernovas and Supernova Remnants"
http://chandra.harvard.edu/photo/category/snr.html

Dozens of images of supernovae taken by the Chandra satellite can be downloaded or printed at this site. One especially interesting one is a picture of the remnant of the supernova seen by Tycho Brahe in 1572.

Max Planck Institute for Gravitational Physics: "Einstein-online: Gravitational Deflection of Light"
http://www.aei.mpg.de/einsteinOnline/en/spotlights/light_deflection/index.html

> *This site provides an excellent animated illustration of how the sun's gravity affects the apparent position of a star.*

McMurray University: "Galileo and the Mathematics of Motion"
http://www.mcm.edu/academic/galileo/ars/arshtml/mathofmotion1.html

> *This site provides an outstanding illustration of how historians believe Galileo arrived at his relationship between time and distance.*

Physics at Syracuse University: "Kepler's Second Law: A JAVA Interactive Tutorial"
http://www.phy.syr.edu/courses/java/mc_html/kepler_frame.html

> *Play with the controls of this Java applet to see Kepler's second law of planetary motion in action.*

"Assignment Earth: Tidal Power."
http://www.youtube.com/watch?v=QHwt5taRsas

> *This video clip shows divers installing tide-powered turbines in New York's East River. The city is pioneering the use of tidal flows to generate electric power.*

"Prelude to Einstein's Theory: The Michelson-Morley Experiment"
http://www.youtube.com/watch?v=ZMdpyisUraY&feature=related

> *This educational video explains the Michelson-Morley experiment with well-done graphics. It also shows why it was the "Prelude to Einstein's theory."*

Picture Credits

Index

About the Author

Phillip Manning is the author of six previous books and 200 or so magazine and newspaper articles. Two of his books—*Atoms, Molecules, and Compounds* and *Chemical Bonds*—were published as part of Chelsea House's Essential Chemistry series. Another book, *Islands of Hope*, won the 1999 National Outdoor Book award for nature and the environment. Manning has a Ph.D. in physical chemistry from the University of North Carolina at Chapel Hill. His Web site www.scibooks.org lists new books and book reviews about science.

Manning would like to thank Jesse Miner, who read and commented on the manuscript. Miner is completing his thesis for a Ph.D. in astrophysics at the University of North Carolina at Chapel Hill. He corrected errors and offered sound advice on how to present the general theory of relativity.